Terry,

There have been few...
who I found to be a
with my heart. You, my
friend, are such a man.

Thanks for your continued
friendship and support.

Prayers for you as you
down this season of life.
God is with you. May you
hear the whispers of the
Holy Spirit as He guides
you. You Matter.

Your Friend,
John Edwards

DESPITE ME

DISCOVER A PROVEN PATHWAY
TO A LIFE OF PASSION AND PURPOSE

JOHN EDWARDS

PRAISE

I have known John Edwards for several years and have been impacted by his friendship and my work with him at Life Quest Seminars. When John asked me to review his book, *Despite Me*, I considered it an honor. I knew John was a man of character, wisdom, and an artful communicator but did not know him as an author.

John's book was riveting and timely. While hopelessness grips many, as so much uncertainty exists among us all, in a way, we as a world have never known, John's book encourages, challenges, and provokes, and above all, gives hope. *Despite Me* wakes us up to see our dreams more prominent than our memories, more significant than our setbacks, and energizes the reader to believe in the limitless life waiting for them.

Despite Me is a MUST read. Way to go, John!

Dr. Russ Irwin BA (Hons) MA PhD
Author, International Speaker, Consultant

Author John Edwards' premise captivated me. It proposes the BIG people who raise us have a significant role in forming who we become and the beliefs we have about ourselves. In *Despite Me*, Edwards guides us through the life journey of Jake. Like many, Jake navigates through numerous struggles in his life, most of them created because of the lies he has come to believe about himself because of the BIG people. He ultimately comes to a fork in the road in his life, one that leads him to unveil a life of significance—one filled with joy, peace, love, acceptance, courage, and worthiness. Jake's story reminds all of us what can be if we only make room for it.

Aleta Norris, Author of *Women Who Spark:*
12 Steps to Catapult Happiness, Cultivate Confidence,
and Discover the Purpose of Your Life

I have had the privilege to count John as a mentor, both through the entire personal development seminar series, where I first met him—through to this very day. As a student, I experienced him later in his journey. Honestly, I figured he had always been such a significant connector, caring man, and a highly emotionally intelligent person. Getting to know his backstory only has me more in awe of the path he has been on to get here. During the seminar, I had always been so focused on my own experience as it was hard even to imagine what the facilitators were experiencing and how they got where they were. *Despite Me* not only gave me some beautiful reminders of games we played but even more, a fuller recollection of what it all meant. Wherever you are on your journey, I recommend bringing John with you!

Susan Anderson, Author:
www.VestedBeauty.com

I first met John Edwards as a facilitator in a personal development setting. I dreamed of being a personal fitness trainer and had no confidence in believing I could achieve the dream. I thought if I could figure out how to do it, then I would be happy. John created a safe, nonjudgmental environment to explore what was holding me back from being happy. What I discovered was I had many people to forgive and, most importantly, myself. John's training spoke to me at a level that opened my eyes to realize I had choices, and suffering is optional. Learning these things has changed my perspective completely. It opened my mind to possibilities that far exceeded my original goal of becoming a personal fitness trainer and being happy.

Despite Me is a relatable read. Some of the obstacles presented are things we all can relate to, and some are shocking and unexpected. John's sheer will to keep moving forward despite the challenges and the journey of how he came to be an accepting, forgiving, and loving person are inspiring. An excellent read for anyone who is seeking answers to make changes in their own lives.

Suzie DeBar, DeBar Fitness and Wellness, LLC, Trainer and Master Coach of NLP, Physique Fitness Trainer

I have come to know to whom much is given, much is required. John Edwards is a man with extraordinary gifting. For anyone looking to grow by identifying constraints to expanding their influence through effective leadership, John's book, *Despite Me*, is a must read. This book is a gift to humanity. It helps people discover their complexity while delivering breakthroughs and transformational revelations that contain the power to change one's life and direction—setting you up for the potential for new encounters and achievements not possible before renewing your mind, which is the book's primary objective. I recommend this book to anyone willing to take the journey of discovery into themselves!

Lowell (Skip) Olmstead,
CEO Strategic Cultural Initiatives

Author John Edwards is a man of real character and integrity, whom I admire, trust, and respect greatly. His honesty, vulnerability, and care for others is evident in the stories he shares throughout *Despite Me*. Beginning with the introduction, John captivates the reader with an honest and open way of sharing the story of his life experiences. If you are looking for a relatable, heartfelt experience toward creating positive change in your life, this is the book to read! He openly invites his reader to compare and reflect on their journey while sharing his own. *Despite Me* challenges the reader to step outside their comfortable norm and take a chance on a new, more significant trajectory in all aspects of their life. This book is full of heart, written intriguingly with the necessary tools to create what you want most in your life.

Lisa Miller, Founder of Fur-Ever Loved Animal Rescue

John is a seasoned "real" person who has walked through a life of challenges and setbacks that would have been catastrophic to many. However, being the guy who not only persevered but ended up thriving on these challenges by having grit as well as a healthy dose of compassion for humanity. I know God used his previous walk to sharpen his sword to become the facilitator, mentor, teacher, and Yoda-like advisor who has blessed me and so many others. He helped me and the healthcare business I ran to reach for abundance and achieve business objectives I thought impossible. This book is an extraordinary blessing to share his wisdom with so many more business leaders and individuals than he has already touched by his previous work.

R. Alan Gleghorn
President and co-owner, Strat Tech Solutions, LLC

Some people come into your life who have a lasting impression. For myself, John Edwards was one of those people that not only created a lasting impression but changed my life in incredibly significant ways. When I first met John, I must admit I didn't like my first impression. He was a facilitator in a leadership training course I was taking. Looking back, I have learned to understand I was one alpha male looking at another as a challenge. John is not only a very accomplished alpha male but he has the biggest heart and desire to help everyone around him to be aware, act, and live to the fullest capability of their being-ness. I am delighted to endorse his book, *Despite Me*. John, in my view, is an unequaled tower of strength to life coaching and leadership building. His insight into human behavior is expansive and impressive.

Dr. Raul Garcia, 2020 WA, State Gubernatorial Candidate, Medical Staff President, Lourdes Medical Center, Director of Emergency Medicine, Lourdes Medical Center, WA ACEP Board of Directors

John's story's raw authenticity shows us how the complexities of life, from troubling valleys to the seemingly mundane to the mountain highs, have a profound and lasting influence on who a person will become. His could be anyone's story, and the peek into the depths of his experience takes the reader on a profound, deeply moving journey of self-discovery, self-awareness, and ultimately love and forgiveness. With aplomb, compassion, and a deep love of humanity, John Edwards brings the reader through the experience of examining their own life through his story to discover and overcome that something has been preventing an entirely free life.

Laura Smyer, Lead Facilitator Life Quest Seminars, Co-Creator Beauty Revealed And The Butterfly Affect, Speaker, Leadership and Personal Coach, Senior Facilitator Learning and Development with Molina Healthcare

John Edwards is an excellent example of taking your past, reframing it, and using it for good to help others overcome their history and the obstacles they think stand in their way. John is bold, real, and authentic in the way he teaches. It is encouraging to see where John has come from and how he applied these principles to his own life, how far he has come, and the man he is today. John is gracious, kind, and never judges. He helps you look deep within to heal from your past and embrace your inner child so you can become all you want. Thank you, John, for stepping out and into your greatness, helping so many others discover their own authentic heart.

Michelle Klaseen, Author, Speaker, Certified Coach in
Your Secret Name, A Deeper Path, and *Unhackable,*
Life Quest Seminars Facilitator

DESPITE ME

DISCOVER A PROVEN PATHWAY
TO A LIFE OF PASSION AND PURPOSE

JOHN EDWARDS

Published by Author Academy Elite
P.O. Box 43, Powell, OH 43035
AuthorAcademyElite.com

Visit the author's website at www.lifequestseminars.com

For quantity book orders, please contact the author directly at:

support@lifequestseminars.com

Paperback: 978-1-64746-708-1
Hardback: 978-1-64746-709-8
Ebook: 978-1-64746-710-4

Library of Congress Control Number: 2021902022

Editing by: Marvin Wilmes and Tina Morlock

DEDICATION

To my incredibly patient and loving wife of 52 years, Linda King Edwards, you have had my back in more ways than I can count. You have believed in me, supported my dreams and goals, cheered me on when I felt like quitting, and loved me through some of the most difficult times of our relationship. You, my love, are the ROCKSTAR of my life and the lynchpin of our marital union.

To my children, Kimberly and Michael, your forgiveness and love is a gift I cherish. To have the kind of relationship we have built together has made me a better man, friend, mentor, and father. I love you each differently albeit with a father's love that is accepting, compassionate, forgiving, and understanding. I believe in you and know God's plan for you each is being manifested in your hearts.

To the thousands of participants who risked their time, finances, and emotions to sit in a workshop or seminar where I was a Facilitator: thank you for trusting me to guide you through an incredibly challenging process so you, too, had the opportunity for revelation and breakthrough that led you to more satisfaction and fulfillment and a life of passion and purpose.

In honor of my living God and my Lord and Savior, Jesus Christ, your never-ending love, mercy, and grace strengthens me daily. Your forgiveness fuels me to continue forward, setting ego aside and being your hands and feet to reach more people. Your written word in Proverbs 23:7: "For as he thinks in his heart, so is he" drives me daily to become a better man."[1] From Romans 12:2: "Do not be conformed to this world, but be transformed by the renewing of your mind" is my North star that guides my mission of generational transformation.[2] And from Luke 6:45: "For out of the abundance of the heart, the mouth speaks" has turned my hardened heart into one filled with love overflowing, so much so, I cannot give it all away, no matter how hard I try.[3]

NOTE TO THE READER

For every reader who is seeking something greater from life while looking for ways to overcome your childhood trauma, let the lessons of this book, *Despite Me*, and the story of its main character, Jake, guide you to a far better way to create your life, live passionately from purpose, and be filled with love. It doesn't have to be hard, yet it can be elusive without a guide who has overcome and is reaching back to give you a hand. Through my book, *Despite Me*, I am offering you the hand of an experienced guide. Take my hand!

TABLE OF CONTENTS

INTRODUCTION

Twenty years ago, I set out on a quest to learn what great leaders were, how they developed, and how they maintained their leadership style when all hell breaks loose. During my more than 30 years in leadership—where two or more gathered, I was always the leader—I thought my style was effective. As a manager in the lumber and wood products industry in the Northwest, I managed budgets and resources in several plants—oversaw hundreds of workers and supervisors, negotiated with union business agents, dealt with logging companies and longshoremen, conceptualized—and managed the building of the manufacturing plants themselves: all great things, or so I thought, until I was no longer needed.

Despite Me is a journey about how I came to learn who I thought I was as a man, husband, father, leader, and the man who the world perceived was 180 degrees off on my compass. My quest led me to life-transforming discoveries that shook my core beliefs, so much so, I opened myself up to a process of character transformation that turned my life of existence from feeling like a dead man walking into a life of passion and purpose.

My readers have an advantage. My journey may be much like their journey. I have lived in and crossed the great desert of life and transformed my character in the quest. Here within *Despite Me*, I provide my readers with tools, techniques and, approaches for shifting their fixed, victim, and scarcity mindsets and limiting beliefs so they, too, can live their life as God intended for them.

Some of the names of the characters within *Despite Me* have been changed to protect the anonymity of each person and the families of those now departed from this earth.

PART I
DEAD MAN WALKING

I

HOW DID HE GET HERE?

Pain is inevitable. Suffering is optional.

—Haruki Murakami

Most people will go to their graves never reaching their life's full potential nor realizing all their heart's desires, dreams, and goals. It seems insane to think the things they would never achieve would make this world such a fantastic place to live. All the music, books, inventions, and science humanity should bring forth would go to the grave. Why is it so common amongst all of humanity that a being has free will and the ability to collaborate with others to create more—be more, give more, love more—and live life from a mindset of abundance with passion and purpose?

Everyone is born into an existing family culture. For some, their culture is filled with childhood trauma passed down by the parents and experienced by them. It has been known for hundreds of years that a child's unconscious mind is 95% programmed and operates from these deep-seated programs by the age of seven. Included are harmful emotional programs the child may have encountered and experienced while in the womb. These programs lie dormant until the right trigger activates them.

When you live in a culture of broken and wounded humans surrounded by victims who live with poverty and scarcity mindsets, there doesn't seem to be any viable alternative. Fate deals you a hand, and it's the only hand you get to play throughout your life. You're not self-aware enough to know you are operating from mindsets—worldviews— that aren't your own but, rather, those of your parents, teachers, and those who had authority over you as a child. As adults, we try to fill a massive hole with any external thing— relationships, houses, new jobs, new cars, addictions—but nothing lasts, and you move on to the next thing you hope will be the final missing link. You don't trust or love deeply. You don't believe in yourself, take risks, or do any of the things that would provide you a lifetime of satisfaction and fulfillment. You live an exhausting life, and you feel as though you are taking up space and sucking up oxygen. You have become a dead man walking.

After decades of facilitating and coaching thousands of people from across the globe who suffer from victim and scarcity mindsets, I have discovered many reasons we humans fall into the trap and will share life experiences along with steps for overcoming these fixed mindsets and worldviews.

My request is you remain open-minded and explore for yourself and determine if what I have discovered to be true in those I have coached and trained may also be true for you. The lessons and tools I will reveal when applied to your life can help you transform your life from where you are into life as it was meant to be lived—abundant, joy-filled, fun, passionate, loving, loved, valued, with purpose—and so much more. If your life is not full of these qualities, you will want to learn all about these discoveries and integrate many of the lessons and strategies into your mind. You should renew your mind, the part of you that operates unconsciously but doesn't always serve your highest good.

Let's begin from a common starting point to get the full picture of how people can arrive at a time in life where they may know a change must occur, or something unthinkable could happen. Stories differ, but your wounds have common threads that pierce the heart, burying your passion, purpose, and creativity under many layers of pain and anger.

Starting with a difficult birth can often set a person up for a difficult life journey. During the 1950s, being born at home was bad enough, but to be born breach without medical help was especially traumatic on the child's system.

Years earlier, Bertha had lost a child on its day of birth because she was at home alone. Not being able to take care of her newborn girl, she held her baby in her arms while hemorrhaging, almost bleeding to death, as her baby died.

Thirteen years later, a baby boy would be born into this family culture where scarcity, poverty, and victimhood were not only typical, but it was their way of life. Beginning on his day of birth, the boy would become the ninth victim of this family's limiting beliefs, growing up believing he had no options or choices to live any differently than his parents. Buying into his parents' limiting mindsets and developing his own during his formative years, the boy grew into a man who believed life was a struggle and a fight for survival. He would learn to master the art of struggling to survive. But let's examine how this man's life could be a mirror in many ways of your life, and the struggles you have lived with and are ready to break free from.

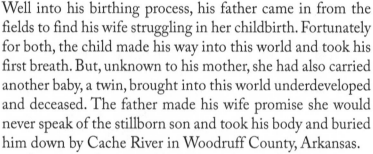

Well into his birthing process, his father came in from the fields to find his wife struggling in her childbirth. Fortunately for both, the child made his way into this world and took his first breath. But, unknown to his mother, she had also carried another baby, a twin, brought into this world underdeveloped and deceased. The father made his wife promise she would never speak of the stillborn son and took his body and buried him down by Cache River in Woodruff County, Arkansas.

As a man, Jake would never understand why his twin being born deceased had to be a secret; it seemed to be the way things were back then. His mother and father would keep this secret for decades to come. He only learned about having a twin at the age of 47 following his oldest brother's funeral. The family was together sharing stories like families do at such a time, when someone told a hilarious story, and everyone busted out laughing. When the group quieted down, their mother asked if they would like to hear something funny. Well, of course, everyone said yes, as it seemed to be the time for sharing stories and having fun together. Why she picked this time and especially this time in his life to share her secret, he would never understand. But without so much as softening the blow of her secret, she said, "Jake, you had a twin brother. He came into this world deceased, but he was your twin."

Jake would figure out years later the only people who knew about his twin were his father, mother, and oldest brother, who was 13 years old on the day of Jake's birth. All three had kept their secret, and once his father and oldest brother were gone, his mother felt it was something he should know.

Jake became angry with her for telling him and even resented her for a long time for keeping such important information from him.

<hr>

Life was hard for everyone in the family. They were impoverished and lived in the flatlands of Arkansas, known as tornado alley. His mother worked sunup to sundown in the fields and took care of the household duties when she got home.

His father, a veteran, was not the same man who went to war. Traumatic events of his service in the U.S. Army left him filled with rage and no desire to be the father the family needed. So, he turned to alcohol and ran away after building up more debt than his wife could cover with a single job. Jake's mother worked as a waitress, house cleaner, and farmhand, and she took in laundry for the more affluent people in their community.

Decades later, Jake learned how different his father was before entering the U.S. Army while sorting through his mother's possessions following her death. Jake found neat ribbon-bound war letters his father had written during his six-month hospital stay in England following a near-death injury while he was deployed in Nice, France. The battle was a particularly deadly one, with his father being the only man from his platoon who survived. Before his deployment to France, he had been deployed to campaigns in Africa and Asia, where he was awarded several medals, including the Bronze Star. His father was awarded the Purple Heart for his battle injuries while in Nice, France, before being discharged from the Army in 1945. As a kid, Jake remembered sneaking into his parents' bedroom, finding the medals, and playing with his father's Purple Heart. It felt heavy in his hand, and Jake liked to imagine he was also a war hero injured in battle. His father would never know this about Jake, as he didn't exist in his father's life. His mother had often told him his father didn't want "those damn kids" anyway.

Nightmares haunted him from his time in WWII, and he would spiral down. He suffered from shell shock, and when he was spiraling out of control, he would leave home to find work so he could live away from the family, drinking more and more. His time away would last for months, but he kept coming back, and his wife would forgive him and take him back.

The cycle would repeat itself over and over in their 28-year marriage. While he was home, his father's rage would surface, and he would take it out on his wife and the older children. He once beat the oldest girl with a razor strap for not putting gravy on her biscuits the way he liked them, and other times, he would beat his wife for over or under-cooking his eggs. He was a slave to his rage, and the family paid the price.

From Jake's earliest memory, until his parent's final separation, he watched his father beat his mother down to the ground until she could get her hands on anything to strike back. One day, when Jake and his younger brother, Hank, were outside playing, his mother darted out the front door screaming at his father—who was on a dead run behind her—to stop and leave her alone. She ran to one of the giant trees on the edge of the road. She quickly took refuge on the opposite side of the tree from her husband. Jake and Hank watched as he struck out at her and finally grabbed her arm and dragged her toward him. In a flash, Bertha bent over and picked up a board Jake and Hank had used as a bridge on the tiny dirt road they had formed where they were playing with cars. In one single swing, she struck his side with the kind of force a logger might use while chopping down a tree. Jake and Hank heard the crunch of their father's ribs and the whooshing sound as he heavily exhaled.

Bertha broke free as Jake's father was distracted by his pain. She ran across the street to the neighbor's house, where the chief of police lived. Shortly after, a police car arrived, and the officer put Jake's father in handcuffs and the police car's back seat. Had his father been drinking heavily, he would have easily fought off a single officer. There were times as many as eight officers were needed to bring his drunk father under control. On this occasion, however, his father complied with the officer without resisting. Jake and Hank were terrified. Seeing their father hauled away in handcuffs, they wondered if they would ever see him again.

To make money, Jake's mother would pick cotton planted in the rich black dirt in the river bottomlands of Woodruff County. Farmers planted hundreds of acres of cotton and needed as many pickers as they could hire. Early in the morning, a truck would pick the family up and take them to the cotton fields. There were wooden benches in the truck's bed and an old tarp used for a cover. It would flap so loudly from the wind having a conversation was impossible.

One of the pickers, an older woman with a large dark-colored wide brim hat, would always sit closest to the truck's tailgate. As they made their way to the cotton fields, this old woman would spit her liquefied snuff out the back of the truck. Jake's father dipped snuff, so the smell of it and her spitting it out was nothing new to him. The difference was this old woman would put two snuff-stained fingers to her lips and spit between them. The kids strained to watch her spit to see how far the truck had gone before the spit hit the ground. She would look back at the kids and laugh, and the kids would laugh with her.

Jake was five years old when his mother made a cotton sack he could pull behind him. His mother taught all her kids how to grab the cotton from the inside of the cotton bolls so the hull's needle sharpness—pointed straight up like the tip of a spear—would not prick their fingers. They would have to learn this lesson over and over before they would get through a day without screaming out in pain from a finger poke from a cotton boll tip. Along with all the other pickers, she and her children would choose to work in a row. They would stand at the beginning of the row and wait for the sunrise to provide enough light so they could pick the cotton in their row.

The heat of the sun warmed up the fields and brought the diamondback rattlesnakes out. Jake's mother warned them to keep a sharp eye out for the snakes and to call her if they saw one. His mother carried a short-handled hoe with her she would use to chop a snake in two. She was accurate with her swing, usually chopping off the snake's head. Once the sun illuminated the rows, everyone began to pick the cotton and stuff it into their bags. After picking for a while, the cotton in the sack needed to be shaken down to make more room. The first few times, Jake's mother showed him how to raise his sack as high as he could reach and shake it, moving the cotton lower and lower toward the bottom. Her children quickly learned her technique.

It would seem like they had picked for hours by the time they reached one of the cotton wagons the farmers had placed throughout the fields. Jake's mother would come to her children's cotton row and take their sacks, empty them into hers, then take it to the weighmaster at the wagon. The weighmaster would weigh the cotton sack, hanging each load from a mechanical spring scale that hung off the wagon's side. The scale spring would squeak as the full sack of cotton pulled down to a measure of weight indicated on the scale's dial so the weighmaster could record the weight in his little book. Then, another man in the wagon would hoist the sack into the wagon and dump it out, throwing the empty sack back to the owner. Between weighing the sacks and dumping them, both men would stomp the cotton down into the wagon so they could load as much as possible before a tractor came to haul it to the cotton gin.

Bertha's children had no idea why she added their cotton to hers. Jake was an adult before his mother told him her reason for having her kids in the field picking alongside her. There wasn't anyone to watch Jake, Hank, and his two older sisters, Mary and Gail, during the day while she picked cotton, so she took them to the cotton fields. The farmers paid the men 40 cents for every hundred pounds of cotton harvested but only paid the women ten cents for the same cotton weight. If Jake's mother hadn't taken her children's pickings and added them to hers, she would need to pick four times the amount of cotton the men picked to get paid an equal amount of money. As children, they didn't think about such things, but Jake's mother intended on making as much money as possible to care for and feed her family. She could out pick any man or woman in the field but still needed her children's cotton to get paid maximum wages.

Every picker would pick a full row of cotton, with his mother backtracking from time to time to catch her children up with her row. When the sun got high in the sky, Jake's mother would unpack the lunch she had finished making before the truck picked them up for the ride to the cotton fields. His mother carried the lunch and a gallon jar of water with her so she didn't have to waste time going back to the truck. They ate their lunches in the field and quickly returned to picking cotton.

The rows seemed as long as the distance to the horizon. Once they reached the end of a row, they would move over to the next available row and pick back to the wagon. His mother repeated the process of transferring their cotton to her sack, getting weighed and recorded in the little book the weighmaster kept in his bib overall pocket. Everyone could only pick when there was enough sunlight to light the way. As daylight dimmed, they returned to the truck for the ride home, stopping and letting other pickers off along the way.

After a full day of picking cotton, Jake's mother would fill their large steel tub with hot water she had heated on the stovetop after bringing in pail after pail of water from the outside well pump. The kids would strip off their dirty clothes from the day and bathe, two at a time, in the tub. Jake's mother made sure they didn't take any shortcuts in the tub by finishing them up with a quick scrub with lye soap and a cloth so they were squeaky-clean. After dressing her children, his mother prepared and cooked dinner. Everyone ate dinner together, then his mother and the older girls would wash the dishes and put them away. Once it was all taken care of, his mother would iron the previous day's wash while she boiled the white clothes to get them cotton white.

People from all around knew Bertha's whites would win first prize if there were such a thing. Even though they were poor, his mother took great pride in her work and made sure she had the whitest whites around. Before his mother would go to bed, she would start their lunches for the next day in the fields. Sometimes, she wouldn't get to bed until close to midnight, then she would rise before anyone else to make breakfast, finish making lunches, and dress the kids for another day in the cotton field.

———— ⊶⊷ ————

During one of his father's times away, he wrote to his wife and said he was coming home and moving the family to southern California. In his letter, he told her his brothers, Walt and Mutt, had great jobs, and there was lots of work in agriculture. He persuaded his wife to move with stories of milk and honey flowing everywhere.

It was 1958 when Jake's mother packed everyone into a blue 1953 Buick sedan, including her feather mattress, and the family left Arkansas. As kids, it was all adventure for Jake and Hank. They had never seen colorful neon signs before and marveled at the sight of them. The car kept having engine fires, which his father had to put out, then repair the engine wiring before they could drive on. After days of driving, the family finally made it to a desert town called Westmorland in Imperial Valley, California.

It was a town with buildings in the oldest section so old the residents no longer painted them, and it was mostly uninhabited. In its boom days, celebrities from up north of the valley—Palm Springs, Indio, and surrounding areas— would come down to this little sleepy town and spend time there because of gambling and available women of the evening. Jake's father had already been there to find work and a place to move his family. He had rented a three-bedroom duplex, provided by the Imperial County Housing Authority. They were poor people who moved into a poor neighborhood.

Jake grew up seeing his mother work three to five jobs during a week to feed, clothe, and provide housing for her family. When he was home, his father also worked multiple jobs at southern California's farms, and the family didn't see him much of the time.

———— ∞∞∞ ————

Jake entered the California elementary school system in the second grade. He was a small-framed boy and had a funny accent—coming from Arkansas—and the other kids made fun of him. He never really understood why, but some of the older boys would gang up on him and beat him up. It happened so often he was afraid to go out to recess or be caught out of the classroom by himself. Often through his grade school years, a gang of boys would chase Jake into the boy's restroom, beat him to the floor, push him off into the floor urinal, and stomp on him. The school principal paddled him for fighting and called his mother to come and get him. His mother became so frustrated she would whip Jake before escorting him back across the street to the school.

Before entering high school, Jake made a vow he would rather die than be embarrassed or humiliated ever again. The vow changed his thinking, his *mindset*, and him. He would live it out daily. No longer was he the runt who couldn't take care of himself. Although he had not grown physically, his mindset had shifted, so he became a fierce brawler. After making the vow, Jake would never lose another fight, whether with one, two, or ten boys. He would use whatever means necessary to make sure he walked away. After all, he had watched his mother fight off his father dozens of times, and she used anything she could reach as a weapon.

From looking at pictures in books, Jake learned French boxing and the foot-fighting style known as Savate. He was fast and able to kick high on his opponent's body and head. With a single, accurately placed kick, Jake could knock a boy, of most any height, to the floor, which was generally enough to get them to run off. He made sure his mother bought him new shoes with hard soles, making his kick blow as effective as possible. During his high school days, different boys pulled guns on Jake, and each time, with lightning speed, Jake took the gun away and beat the boy over the head with it. He beat one boy so severely he was reported to the high school principal.

Once the principal heard the other boy had pulled a gun on Jake, the principal told both to get back to their classroom and stop causing problems. Jake assumed the principal either kept the gun or disposed of it because he never heard from the police, and his mother didn't ask about the fight.

Jake had experienced what it was like to be in control and feel powerful, and he wanted to experience it more and more. Living close to the Mexican border, Jake and his friends would cross over on the weekends, drink beer, and look for someone to fight. They were all crazy to think they could live forever but felt like they had nothing to lose.

LOOKING BACK:

Even as a young man, Jake was undergoing a transformation he didn't fully understand. His thinking was evolving. Before, he didn't see he had any choices and made choices that didn't always serve his highest good. But he was beginning to feel he was more and more in control. Isn't that what everyone wants to achieve, a feeling of being in control?

What is being in control? Does it mean you can do, be, and have anything you desire? Does it mean your life is your own to make of it what you want? Control is an illusion humans strive for but never seem to achieve, at least consistently.

The person you are today is the result of a culmination of significant emotional life experiences, other people's judgments you own, behaviors, chosen and programmed values, and millions of choices you have made, beginning from early in your childhood. Of course, no baby is consciously making choices, but there is a point in time when a child experiences love and support when he or she cries out. Receiving this kind of attention, something from an external source becomes what the child soon learns to want more and more.

Somewhere around the age of eight, children develop a level of self-awareness and begin to create their personality based on what they need from the prominent people who are caring for them. So, the child, unconsciously, creates a pose for each thing they seek from these people. In one case, it might be a pose of creativity to get positive attention and accolades, while another pose might be knowledgeable to obtain acceptance or approval.

Regardless, the child will use these poses, unconsciously, to numb the pain of childhood trauma. When I use the term trauma, I mean parental, sibling, or other family member abuse at any level: sexual molestation, bullying, mental distress, parental emotional shutdown, or abandonment, to name some of the traumas a child might experience. To the child, his or her trauma and subconscious emotional connection to the trauma is as severe as another child's trauma. The physical manifestations may look completely different, but the emotional and mental scarring is as deep because pain is pain, whether brought on by words or other means.

YOUR INTROSPECTIVE CHALLENGE:

1. How do elements of Jake's story mirror your story?

   _____

   _____

   _____

   _____

2. What are some of the emotional and mental scars you can see in Jake? How are his scars like yours?

   _____

   _____

   _____

   _____

3. What are some of the poses—acts, pretenses, facades, masquerades—you are aware of using to gain something from others such as acceptance, love, approval, admiration, feeling valued, etc.? What do you hope to achieve?

   _____

   _____

   _____

   _____

4. What dominant character traits can you attribute to your limiting decisions, beliefs, fixed mindsets, or worldviews you know are holding you back and keeping you from playing a larger game of life?

   _____

   _____

   _____

   _____

II

WORLDVIEWS DETERMINE OUR RESULTS

It is hard to convince a high-school student that he will encounter a lot of problems more difficult than those of algebra and geometry.

—E. W. Howe

What is a worldview? A worldview is a philosophy or conception made up of subconscious programming, such as limiting decisions, limiting beliefs, scarcity, and a victim and poverty mindset. One person's worldviews may be more growth-oriented, and another person may have such a narrow worldview they leave no room for any other input. Jake was an individual who came from a victim and poverty-minded culture, so he tended to operate from the latter. Worldviews are deep-seated, unconscious programs individuals take ownership of during their formative years. Children have much of their unconscious mind programmed from birth to the age of seven by their exposure to significant negative and positive emotional experiences. These can include parents, grandparents, teachers, siblings, other relatives, and those who have or take authority over us. Beyond age seven, the subconscious mind's programming continues, making our teen years even more difficult. So, how does one even begin to create a life of significance and fulfillment when our *operating system*—our subconscious—seems to be wired for self-sabotage?

When Jake was 14, he worked after school and on the weekends for the local grocery store. The owner was a kind man who took him on and showed him how to do many things in the store. He learned how to restock the shelves, clean the floors, restock the freezers, and fill coolers with milk, beer, and soft drinks. He knew how to clean behind the meat counter and paid close attention to how the owner would take a side of beef and break it down into all the different meat cuts. There were steaks, roasts, ribs, trimmings for grinding (which was used for the hamburger), stew meat, soup bones, and all the pieces the poor could afford to buy: tripe, goat heads, fish heads, liver, pigs' feet, chicken feet, beef soup bones, and so much more.

It wasn't long before the owner had Jake grinding the trimmings for the hamburger. Jake mixed various trimmings and bull meat, a very dark red meat, to get the right color and mix of lean and fat meat that sold quickly, both to the public and local restaurants. He learned how to cut up poultry, use the meat slicer for cold cuts, clean and slice beef liver, clean the meat case, and prepare it for the next day. The owner taught him how to sharpen all the knives and use and change the band saw used for cutting ribs and steak with the bone in them. Showing ultimate trust in him, the owner taught him how to run the register and check out their patrons' groceries. There were no computers then. It was all hand keyed into the register, which meant Jake had to memorize all the pricing in the store. Jake felt valued, and his confidence soared.

Then one day, a woman, Dorothy, who Jake had seen in the store from time to time, came to the meat counter with her five small children tagging along behind her. She ordered several cuts of meat, which Jake weighed carefully and wrapped with great precision. She moved on and finished her shopping, by which time Jake was back at the front of the store sacking the other patrons' groceries.

She arrived at the front of the store so Jake could check her out. Once he had her groceries sacked up, he helped carry them to her car and loaded them into the backend of her station wagon. She seemed especially grateful for this as she had to herd her five children into the car on such a hot, 120-degree day in the valley.

Over the weeks, Dorothy would return and seek Jake out to help her in different parts of the store, and Jake willingly helped. Her small children were always with her, and he felt she needed help to manage them and her shopping. Then one day, she came in by herself to do her shopping. She asked Jake if he could help her get her groceries home, saying she would quickly bring him back. The owner knew her and said it would be okay. Jake traveled a mile or so in her car and helped carry the groceries in the house.

As they were about to leave, she said, "I'm going to be opening the pool tonight, and if you want, and if your mother will let you, come over and swim." The pool was open to the public during the day, and on occasion, it was available at night.

Jake hadn't noticed her at the pool before, even though he lived only a couple of blocks away. It turned out she was one of the lifeguards, and she could open the pool at night if she wanted.

Swimming was one of the easiest and most popular ways to cool down from the valley heat. Jake and the other poor kids liked the pool because their families couldn't afford central cooling. Jake's family had a desert cooler, a metal box with a massive blower fan, and straw mat filters. Water from the city lines connected to the box would flow over straw filters while the large blower would move air over the straw mat and into the house. When it was 120 degrees outside, the coolest place inside was the concrete slab floor covered in tile. Jake and his brother would lie down on their bedroom floor with their heads sticking into the hallway where the blower would force air into the house. Wearing shorts without a tee-shirt, the cooler air from the desert cooler kept them comfortable throughout the night.

Jake's mother did not have any reason to say no when he asked if he could go swimming, telling her the pool would be open that night. He could see the pool building from his front yard, so he knew when she arrived and opened the pool. Jake generally ran everywhere he went no matter the distance, and this time was no exception. By the time he arrived, everything was open, and she was already swimming.

Jake immediately jumped into the pool, not paying attention to who else was there. When he came back to the surface and looked around, there were no other people present. It did seem strange, but she had opened the door. He swam to the deep end, where she was hanging onto the side. There was a set of iron pipe steps affixed to the pool wall, and the top step was at the right height so he could sit on it and still be more than half under the water.

Dorothy began to talk to him, asking all kinds of questions. Did he have a girlfriend? What else did he like to do? Did he like working at the store? And what Jake thought was a very bizarre question at the time: have you ever made love with a girl? Jake knew what she was talking about because he had heard the older boys talking about sex. He was embarrassed and felt a strange sensation all through his body. He jumped forward, going under the water, and upon resurfacing, he took off swimming to the opposite end of the pool to avoid the question.

As it does in the desert when the sun sets, it got very dark, and they could no longer see to swim. Soon after dark, she said it was time to close and go home, but she would be opening again in a couple of days, and if he wanted, he could come and swim any time. Jake thanked her for opening the pool and inviting him to swim. He loved to swim. Jake often went swimming with his friends in the irrigation canals. The water was always moving and cold, making it a great place to cool off in the desert. Besides, there were watermelon and cantaloupe fields nearby. He and his friends could have a feast eating the hearts from the watermelons and the meat of the cantaloupes, throwing the waste into the canal to hide the evidence should they get caught swimming. Swimming in the canals was against the Imperial Irrigation District's policy, and they had people who would drive around checking the gates and managing the flow. The gates were manual opening, so the tenders were always coming around.

Over the next year and a half, Jake would watch for Dorothy to come to the store. He would make sure he was always available to help her with the groceries and her children. During one of her shopping trips, as they finished putting the groceries in the car, she asked him if he would like to earn some additional money by babysitting her kids for the evening. She had plans to be out for a few hours and would pay him 50 cents each hour. Jake said it would be great if his mother were okay with it. It turned out he did not see his mother as she was waitressing in another town and would not be home until late. Jake arrived at the agreed-upon time, and she introduced him to each of the five children, who were all in their pajamas and ready for bed. The oldest was around ten years old, much too young to babysit, so he understood why she would ask him to sit. Jake asked where her husband was, as he knew she was married. She told him he was on a trip for a few days. She grabbed her purse, told him to raid the refrigerator if he wanted, saying she would be back by eleven, and left. Jake was excited because his family did not have extra food for raiding, and she had a massive television to watch. They had a tiny television at home, and a large family couldn't gather around it easily.

Jake ate snacks and drank soda until he could eat or drink no more. True to her word, she drove up at eleven and came into the house. Jake was expecting to get paid and leave, but she said she wanted to hear how the kids were and all about what he did while she was gone. To Jake, it seemed like they talked for almost an hour when she reached out and pulled him close, kissing him hard. It scared and embarrassed him, but she kept kissing him. Finally, he got loose and said he needed to get home because he could not get his mother's permission, and she would be worried about him. Saying she understood, she paid him and asked if he liked her kissing him. By this time, Jake was 15 years old, and his blood ran hot, and he felt incredible when she kissed him so hard, so he told her he did like her kissing him.

There were many other nights like that over the ensuing months until one night when Dorothy took his hand and led him to her bedroom. Her children were at another babysitter, and they were the only two in the house. She reached out and began to remove his shirt. When he pulled back, she smiled and began to remove her blouse, then bra and skirt. Jake was blown away by seeing a woman's naked body for the first time, and the sensations rushing through his body felt incredible. She was gorgeous for his 15-year-old eyes, and he couldn't resist reaching out to her. Something happened that should never happen to a young, underage boy or girl. She invited him into her bed, giving herself to him in a way he had only heard about from the older boys at school. Jake was molested and raped, but he didn't know it should matter to anyone else; he felt valued and wanted.

Their encounters at the pool and her home continued for more than a year, with sex each time. Jake began to feel much older than he was because he had a sense of control in the relationship. She allowed him to act like a grown man, making decisions, driving her car, and correcting her children. They took trips with the kids to the desert and had picnics with hiking trips. On one trip, the car's front wheels dropped off into a sandpit in the road, getting stuck in the sand. Jake hiked several miles back to a farm to get help. The farmer rescued them, and they made their way back to her house, none the worse off for the experience.

Saturday, as he was sitting in her living room, the door opened, and a large man walked in. He looked at Jake, and without saying a word, the man turned and headed to the back bedroom.

Jake's heart jumped into his throat when he heard the man ask her, "Who is the kid in the living room?"

Jake was shocked at her response. "Jake, he works at the grocery store, and he is babysitting the kids today while I go into town and shop."

They got quiet for a few minutes, and then the man stormed out. Dorothy came to the front of the house and came over to Jake. He asked her, "Who was that?"

"My husband," she said casually. "We are separated and getting a divorce."

Jake was terrified the man would return and kill him.

One night, Jake was babysitting her children when she came home after being out drinking. He was about to leave when a familiar car pulled up.

It was his mother! How did she know he was there? He had not told her he was babysitting. Jake was as scared as he was when Dorothy's husband saw him.

She told him to go out the back and over the fence, and she would tell his mother he had been gone for some time. Jake did not want to go home, so he went to the school's baseball field, hanging out there for a while. When he did get home, his mother was furious, asking him, "Where have you been"? Jake told her he had been walking for a long time and played some at the school ball field. She knew he was lying and started to yell at him about the woman, saying she would get him into trouble if he were not careful. She went for more time than he cared to listen. Jake went to bed angry and scared, thinking his mother would call the police on his girlfriend. She didn't, but they would have to get wiser with when and where they would meet up.

A few months after he turned 16, Jake's mother found out he had been with Dorothy again and blew her top. She threatened to call the police and have her arrested for the rape of a minor. Jake begged her not to, saying they only hung out together, but she was intent on calling them. Jake blew his cool and called his mother a name. "You bitch!" he yelled at the top of his voice. "Why would you do that? We are not hurting anyone, and we love each other."

He had never called his mother a name, and he was sure she would hit him harder than she ever had. She was the only person he could count on, but she ruled with an iron hand, and Jake got something quite different from Dorothy. It was not all sex. She was kind and giving, and Jake felt what he thought was love from her. He sure didn't feel love from his mother, who was generally harsh and controlling, demanding a lot from her children.

All the money Jake made at the grocery store and from working with his friend's father, who was a beekeeper and had hundreds of beehives throughout the valley, was used to help pay the bills. His mother drew welfare but reported every dime Jake made, so it seemed like they could never get ahead. His girlfriend had money and bought food for him when they were together, paid for movie tickets, let him swim for free, and spent time talking with him. Jake felt cared for when he was with her.

But his mother would have none of it and told him he had a choice. He could go to Oregon and live with his older brother, or she was calling the police. Jake was scared for his girlfriend and her children, so he said he would go to Oregon.

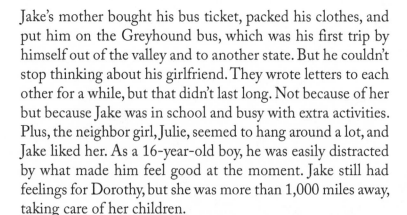

Jake's mother bought his bus ticket, packed his clothes, and put him on the Greyhound bus, which was his first trip by himself out of the valley and to another state. But he couldn't stop thinking about his girlfriend. They wrote letters to each other for a while, but that didn't last long. Not because of her but because Jake was in school and busy with extra activities. Plus, the neighbor girl, Julie, seemed to hang around a lot, and Jake liked her. As a 16-year-old boy, he was easily distracted by what made him feel good at the moment. Jake still had feelings for Dorothy, but she was more than 1,000 miles away, taking care of her children.

Julie was older and paid him a lot of attention. She lived only two houses away, and they talked and laughed together every day. Then, Christmas Eve arrived, and she suggested they deliver bags of goodies to the underprivileged and less fortunate. Though his family fit into her definition, he agreed, and they began to gather up all kinds of goodies and small toys to give to the families. They had so much fun with the project, especially when delivering the bags to the families. Being the new kid in the area without any knowledge of who needed the help, Julie provided the addresses, and he drove his brother's car, and together, they delivered all the goodie bags. Seeing the reactions of the families was so exciting for him. Jake felt like a hero in their lives. They expressed so much gratitude, and he could hardly take it all in. It was such an emotional experience for him.

They finished up and were almost home when she suggested they take a side road, as there was something she wanted to share with him. Not knowing the area, Jake had no idea where this road would take them but soon found out after a couple of miles. They were in the forest on the mountain behind the small city where they lived. The road had turned to gravel, and Jake was afraid of getting stuck at night, so he pulled over to turn around. She asked him to stop and leave the car radio on so they could listen to music. Moments later, she pulled him close and kissed him like Dorothy had, hard and long, putting her tongue in his mouth while she squeezed him tighter against her body. She quickly began to grab at his belt, pulling it apart, then unzipping his jeans. She thrust her hand into his pants so fast he felt out of control. Within moments, she was stripping down, exposing her naked body, and pulling him on top of her. Her passion was over the top, and they stayed there for what seemed like hours.

When they finally did get to her house, she quickly jumped out of the car and ran inside. Not so much as a see you tomorrow, good night, or I had a great time. Jake knew what had happened was much like what he had experienced with Dorothy, but he didn't care. He was getting something important from her, and he wanted to be with her more and more. Jake was 16, and she was 19, so by law, she had committed statutory rape. Once again, Jake was scared to think they would be discovered, and she would get arrested and be in more trouble than could be imagined.

After Christmas Eve, Jake never saw Julie again, even though they lived about a hundred yards apart. Jake learned later, from her brothers, she had left for college shortly after Christmas. Before she would come home on a break, Jake's brother sent him back to California.

One Sunday, after Jake's brother and his wife had returned from church, a familiar car pulled up into the long dirt driveway. *Oh, my God*, he thought. It was his old girlfriend, Dorothy, with her five children and the car packed with everything she could fit, including a carrier strapped on the top of the blue Dodge station wagon. His sister-in-law knew the woman, telling Jake to stay in the house, and she would go out and talk with her. From the living room, Jake could see them talking, and his old girlfriend seemed upset.

Dorothy turned and began walking toward the house. Jake was terrified of what she was going to say and do. The door opened, and she threw something at him and said, "I loved you and thought you loved me." The door closed, she got into the car, and drove away. She had been wearing his class ring around her neck, and she had thrown it at him. Jake never knew what happened to her and the children, although he expected she had moved back to Tacoma, Washington, where she had grown up, as she often spoke of her time there. Jake was never sure he would see her again.

———⌾———

Jake had made friends with Grace, a girl from High School, after returning from Christmas break. Grace had the most beautiful blue eyes, that captured his attention from any place in the choir room. Jake could not take his eyes off her. Then, as fate would have it, they both tried out for the school play. Jake got the part of a husband but to a different girl in school. He later learned Grace was jealous she hadn't gotten the part of his wife. She had missed the day of school when Jake arrived, having enrolled himself after moving from the California desert. From her girlfriend the next day, Grace heard a cute guy from California had moved in and was going to their high school. She was upset with herself, believing another girl already scooped up the cute guy from California. So, when Jake asked Grace if she wanted a ride to play practice, she was completely surprised, saying she would like to ride with him.

For weeks, his brother said they needed a bigger car because there were now four in the household, including his wife, son, and Jake. Jake's income tax refund of $400 was due in the mail, and his brother told Jake he should hand over his refund for a new car because he wasn't paying anything to live with them. Jake didn't want to give up his refund, but when his brother seasoned the offer by giving him the family's Fiat Spider convertible, Jake couldn't resist. Now, you must understand this little red piece of heaven was not in perfect condition. It ran rough, looked worse, and the starter didn't always work, which meant it needed a push to start when it didn't cooperate.

He drove the few miles from his brother's house to Grace's house, which was right in the middle of a youth camp. Her mother and father managed this Christian youth camp on the Oregon coastline.

As Jake drove into the camp, he was surprised to notice this little cottage of a house sitting on a bit of a hill. The roadway led to a garage on the side of the house. An idea popped into his head. If he turned the car around on the top of the roadway and pointed it downhill, then, should it not start quickly, they could roll it down the hill and pop the clutch, which would engage the flywheel, turning the engine over, and the vehicle would startup. His little red Fiat Spider had a four-speed, manual transmission with a clutch, making it a great date car for a young teenager.

On his first date with Grace, she invited him inside to meet her parents, brother, and sisters. *Wait, why am I being introduced to the entire family?* he wondered. *This is only a ride to play practice, nothing more.* And he would bring her straight home afterward because the little beach town rolled up its sidewalks shortly after sunset. Her family was vastly different from Jake's. He felt an uneasiness being with them in their living room with her. After a quick visit, Jake said they would be late for practice if they did not leave right away.

Well, as one might have guessed, on the night he picked her up for play practice, his little red Spider would not start. As quickly as Jake said the car would need a push to start it, she jumped out and gave it a shove, as if she had done it many times before. The vehicle rolled down the hill a few feet before Jake popped the clutch, and the engine roared to life. He hit the brakes, and she jumped in, laughing so hard Jake started laughing with her. The ride to the high school was quick, as they focused on each other rather than the short ride.

After practice, Jake drove the few miles back to the camp, but before they got there, Grace asked him to take a side road, almost across the street from the camp. The road was short and brought them right up to the beach. The sun had not fully set so they could see its beauty, and they walked on the beach, talking about the practice and such other teen interests.

Jake put his hand on her neck and felt her shiver, and she seemed to melt with his touch. It was then Jake knew he would spend the rest of his life with her.

Jake's brother and sister-in-law had invited a young man from a different high school to live with them because he kept getting into trouble. His parents owned a used furniture store where his sister-in-law had purchased all the furniture in the house. They could not afford to buy new, so she got to know the owner's wife well, and when she learned of the problem they were having with their son, she invited them to let him move in with them.

Jake liked Doug as a friend. He was quiet, not intrusive, played the tenor saxophone, and had a decent voice for singing. Jake's brother liked old Christian hymns, so the two boys would sing hymns from an old hymnal without musical instruments. Their harmony sounded amazing. Doug didn't live with them very long before Jake learned what his issues were. He was an alcoholic who drank in secret every day.

Doug would buy beer and hide it in the toilet water tank, and before school, he would drink several cans before catching the bus. He took cans of beer to school and drank them in the bathroom or locker room when no one was around. At night, after they had family time, he would go on a walk and drink while away. Then, Jake learned Doug's father was supplying most of the beer. He also was an alcoholic and saw nothing wrong with giving beer to his son as he walked to the bus pickup area or left a six-pack hidden along the way.

Grace introduced Doug to Debbie, her best buddy since grade school. The two of them hit it off, and they began to spend time together. They double-dated, and when Jake's brother and sister-in-law were gone at night, they would spend time with their girlfriends in his brother's house. It didn't take long before the neighbor told his brother what was going on when they were gone, and his brother confronted him. No matter what Jake said, his brother was not buying it and said he was sending Jake back to California. He had already called their mother and told her about his new girlfriend, and the two of them agreed that sending Jake back was the best option.

On the day Jake was to catch the bus home, Grace came to say good-bye. They both cried and held onto one another, not knowing when they would ever be together again. And then, she told him she was pregnant with their baby. Jake was stunned. *Pregnant with their baby! This could not be happening.* They were too young and didn't have any money. How would they ever be able to raise a child? In those few moments, so many thoughts and questions raced through his mind. Jake knew what he had to do. He had to find a way to return and marry her before the baby was born. There was no question. It was his responsibility to take care of her and raise this baby with her. No matter the cost or sacrifices. Jake knew he was now responsible for a life being born into this world. He would step up and commit to being this child's father in every way. But how would he convince his mother this was the right thing to do?

The bus ride back to California gave him a lot of time to consider his options and how he would broach the subject with his mother. To say she was angry with him would be an understatement. She was even more furious than she was when she learned he had been with Dorothy. Jake's mother told him she would never permit him to marry Grace. And as an underage teenager, she had the power over him to prevent him from getting married. Jake knew, somehow, he must convince her he was committed to fulfilling his responsibility to raise the child and take care of his family. He told her if she did not permit him, he would only leave home and do it anyway.

As a low-income family, they never seemed to have enough money for anything other than the absolute necessities of life: food, shelter, clothing, and a mode of transportation for his mother to get to and from work. But from out of nowhere, Bertha told him she would give him the family's entire savings—$6,000—if he would not do this thing, but, rather, stay home and go to college after his high school graduation.

Bertha said, "I have always thought you were the smartest of all my children, and I don't want to see you ruin your life." What? Why was he now hearing these kinds of words? Had she spoken them to him years earlier, his heart would have melted. For the first time, Jake felt valued by his mother, and a sense of great love poured out of her. His mother was serious! In no uncertain terms, she did not approve of him going back to Oregon to get married. She had convinced him she would never give her permission.

Then, one day, Bertha seemed to have a change of heart and said she would pay for his bus ticket back and would not do anything to stop him from marrying Grace. Jake then realized there was a theme in how she viewed the women his older brothers had married. She didn't like or approve of them either. And his soon-to-be wife would not readily be accepted by his mother as a family member either.

Bertha would refer to her as "that woman" for years to come.

The bus ride back to Oregon seemed to be much faster than he remembered. Maybe it was because he had already seen all the scenery and only had the company of his thoughts. Where would they live? Where would he work? How could he finish school and work? What did her parents think of him? Would her parents give their permission for them to marry? Where could they get married because he was underage? Getting married would be their first big obstacle.

The bus arrived in Portland, Oregon, and Jake's head was pounding. He had stressed over all the questions and fears for the entire bus ride, and a migraine was taking him out. He had arrived several hours early, and Grace could not pick him up until she got off work and asked a friend if she could borrow her car. But his immediate need was to find some aspirin and get rid of the headache. Searching the terminal, Jake couldn't find anything, so he sat in the corner on the floor and cried because the pain was so severe.

Jake had sat there for what seemed like hours when he heard a voice asking, "Are you okay?"

He could barely open his eyes to see a teenage boy standing there looking down at him. Jake told the boy his head was killing him, and he would do anything to get rid of the pain. The boy reached into his pocket and pulled out a small tin, much like what you could buy aspirin in, and handed it to him. The container had a label, Excedrin®, and by pressing the corner opposite the hinge side, Jake opened it. A few pills were left in the tin, but Jake was sure a couple would take care of the pain. As he reached to grab a couple, the boy said, "Hey, you only need one of these. They are stronger than regular aspirin."

So, Jake took only one and swallowed it with the little spit he could gather up in his mouth. The boy took the tin back and said he would see Jake later as he walked away.

It wasn't long before Jake could stand, stretch, and walk about the terminal. His migraine was gone. Jake felt incredible and seemed to have a renewed energy in his body. The teen who had helped him came back around and asked him how he was feeling. Jake told the boy his migraine was gone, and he felt incredible. Jake wanted to walk outside and take in the sights of the city. His new friend agreed, and they took off walking the streets. They hadn't been out for long before a car pulled up, and the boy told Jake the guys in the car were his friends, and they would show Jake the city by car if he wanted. Jake seemed to be more open and trusting than ever and jumped in the back seat. His new friend sat by the door, and the driver drove away from the bus depot. Jake noticed he was sitting between his new friend and a huge man on the other side of the backseat. In the front were two more large men who looked like football players: very muscular.

One of the men in the front began to ask Jake questions, "Where are you from? Why are you here? Did you come by yourself?" He asked so many other questions. Jake finally told them he was going to get married to his girlfriend and raise their new baby together. One of the other men asked him if he had a job, money, and a place to live. Jake pulled out his wallet and showed the man he only had a bus ticket stub and explained they would live with his fiancée's parents for a while.

The men drove around for a long time, asking Jake more and more questions, until one of them spoke out, "There ain't nothing here." The car pulled up to the bus depot, and Jake got out of the vehicle. He watched as the car drove away, and the teen boy waved good-bye.

Not long after his encounter, Grace arrived, driving a gray Dodge Charger. It had a four-speed transmission and was fast running, and Jake wanted to get behind the wheel. He was still feeling like he had incredible energy and was excited to see Grace. She agreed to let Jake drive, and soon, they were on their way to the Oregon coast where she lived. Jake put the car through some trials—burning the tires at a green light, speed shifting—and reaching a top speed on a straight away of 110 miles per hour. And suddenly, Jake realized he was jeopardizing their lives, including his unborn baby's life, and slowed the car down to the speed limit.

In less than two hours, Jake and his girlfriend reached her parent's home. Everything was a blur to Jake—the drive there, how he got over his migraine, the identity of the teen boy, the men in the car, and why he had felt so energized all day long.

LOOKING BACK:

Everyone will experience *defining moments* in his or her lifetime. When attached to negative emotions, many of these moments seem to affect our subconscious programming, and these programs operate automatically in the background of our thinking. At an early age, Jake had a businessman who owned one of two grocery stores in the community notice him. This man would become someone who stood in the gap where Jake's father should have stood. The store owner not only gave Jake a job, but he took the time to teach Jake all he could about his grocery business. This kind of encounter and connection helped Jake increase his self-esteem and his confidence. Jake was trusted with the business's resources and felt he could do no wrong in his employer's eyes.

When Dorothy entered Jake's life, he was already thinking like a much older teen. Whether her influence had anything to do with how she paid attention to him may never be known. However, over a couple of years, she groomed Jake, and he fell victim to her ways. At the right time, and after a long time making Jake feel like he was in control, she committed both an illegal and adulterous act when she raped Jake. This criminal act would alter the course of his life, not always for his highest good. He was too young to be an adult, but he no longer felt like a child.

His encounter at the bus depot had all the trappings of a kidnapping. A teenage boy drugged him at a time his guard was down and lured him into a car filled with grown men who seemed to want something from Jake, but in his state, his only defense was talking incessantly, answering their questions, and filling the moments with nonsensical information. Looking back on the encounter, Jake realized his safety had been in danger, and he was fortunate to walk away.

YOUR INTROSPECTIVE CHALLENGE:

1. As you reflect on the defining moments of your life, how do Jake's moments compare?

    _____

    _____

    _____

    _____

2. Who did you begin to believe you were?

    _____

    _____

    _____

    _____

3. How did your character shift?

    _____

    _____

    _____

    _____

4. What, if any, commitments did you make to yourself that were supported by your shifts?

    _____

    _____

    _____

    _____

III

AS A MAN THINKETH IN HIS HEART

There is little that can withstand a man who can conquer himself.

—Louis XIV

Children begin to, unconsciously, create poses, acts, pretenses, and masquerades to appear a certain way to those who have authority over them. Their childhood negative emotional experiences cause them to seek validation from the big people who are raising them. These validations, such as approval, acceptance, love, and safety, when given, fill a void inside the child who feels broken and wounded. However, as an adult, showing up the same way, he or she produces almost the exact opposite of what the adult seeks from others. Yet the adult goes through life operating from the same worldviews and using the same poses, creating the same mistakes over and over. When an individual's subconscious programming, filtered through their negative emotional experiences, is overriding their conscious thinking, how is it possible for them to create their heart's desires?

The negative emotional experiences of childhood, in many ways, have defined who we believe we are. Once individuals understand how their childhood is foundational to their character development, which determines their limiting beliefs and worldviews, there is hope he or she can transform their character to operate for his or her highest good. Until then, the pain of their negative emotional experiences overrides their conscious decisions, and every area of their life pays a considerable price.

Author, speaker, and trainer Jim Rohn said it well, "You're the average of the five people you spend the most time with."[4] Surely, he meant those you surround yourself with as an adult. However, children spend much of their time with their parents, teachers, and those in authority over them. They absorb the words said to and about them—the acts adults commit and the emotional outbursts the adults express—directly into their unconscious. Hearing over and over the negative comments of childhood—"You'll never amount to anything. Who do you think you are? You can't do that. You're trash. You were an accidental pregnancy. Your father never wanted kids."—become what we settle for in our quest for an abundant and fulfilling life. In so doing, we develop limiting beliefs and fixed mindsets that make those experiences our truths.

Jake and Grace married before he had completed his senior year. Their daughter, Renee, was born, which drove Jake to find employment while still attending school. He tried several jobs, none of which worked out, until he became a caretaker of the youth camp across the street from his in-law's youth camp.

The camp manager, Fritz, was a driven man who set high standards for Jake. He taught Jake the kinds of things a father might teach a young man. Jake felt valued and needed, and as his skills became more developed, Fritz would give him more responsibilities. Making sure a youth camp is ready for the season requires tremendous effort and attention to detail. Every building had to be cleaned top to bottom. Any issues that surfaced from the harshness of the winter months had to receive repairs. The heavy wooden boats in the lake had to be pulled out, cleaned, and painted. Jake would make the floor in the dining lodge shine with a mirror-like reflection. Fritz took great pride in how the camp looked and made sure Jake felt the same way. Jake cut and stacked the firewood for every building that had a meeting space and a large fireplace. He chopped more firewood than he thought campers could use in a season, but there was never much, if any, left in the woodshed at the end of the camping season.

Grace became pregnant with their second child and gave birth to Martin before Renee's first birthday. Having two babies so close together put undue stress on their marriage. Once Jake turned 18, he applied and was hired by one of the sawmills in the county. The pay was much higher than what he earned at the youth camp, but he would be working a late swing shift. Grace would be home alone, taking care of their two babies. Jake never knew what it was like for Grace because he was so focused on his responsibilities. Fearful he could not provide sufficiently for his family, Jake began to work a lot of overtime. When asked, he would always say yes to work the extra hours. In many ways, Jake was doing what his father had done by not being there for his wife or children. He had grown up witnessing the abandonment, and he did not know he could create life any differently.

Jake wanted a promotion to the higher-paying jobs in the sawmill, but the union required the company to put each job opening for bid. Being one of the most recent hires, Jake felt he did not have a chance. After missing out on a few promotions, he decided to take every break and go inside the sawmill and learn as many jobs as he could. Every day for months, he spent his breaks and mealtimes in the heart of the mill practicing until he mastered a position, then he'd move to the next machine and repeat his process of learning.

Finally, a job was posted Jake had mastered, so he bid for the position. To his surprise, the company awarded him the position. It was one of the more physically demanding in the mill and required a great deal of visual awareness and skill. Many of the men working inside the mill were older and did not want to work as hard as the position required. Because he was awarded the position, Jake felt valued and poured himself into performing it perfectly. The position was critical to the flow of lumber in the mill, which required Jake to understand each machine's abilities and its operator. He could maximize the throughput of the mill by managing the flow of the product.

Jake did not stop learning, continuing to practice on the other positions during his break periods. The older men did not seem to mind when Jake would come to their work area as it gave them another break during the shift. After a couple of years of gaining experience in the workflow and desiring promotion, Jake asked his boss if he could learn to operate the head rig, the mill's first log breakdown machine. Jake used his breaks learning how to operate the machine by cutting up logs into slabs that would move through the mill and be processed into lumber. He was a bright and capable young man with a tremendous drive to be and do more with his life.

———— ∞ ————

After working as a union member for a few years, Jake expressed a desire to be trained as a production foreman. His promotions in the mill had allowed him to see the full production floor, and he could spot the bottlenecks his supervisor never addressed. He remembered going home one night, wondering if he had taken too big of a risk by disclosing his inner dream.

Monday morning, Jake received a call from the office telling him the manager wanted to see him. He was completely shocked, and it brought up a level of fear in him he hadn't experienced before. The manager and Jake met with the superintendent and Jake's supervisor to discuss his request to be trained as a foreman. His time with the manager and others went by quickly, and he did not remember a lot about the meeting, but he did remember the manager asking him how bad he wanted the foreman's position. Jake replied, "Like nothing I have ever wanted before."

The manager went on to tell Jake it was a pay cut from his hourly position, which included daily overtime, would he be willing to make such a sacrifice? Without considering what Grace might say, Jake responded with an emphatic yes, he would. The next words out of the manager's mouth floored him. The manager told Jake he would begin immediately as the night foreman. When Jake asked who would train him, the manager's response was shocking. "You already know what to do: keep production at or above current levels, don't allow people to do unsafe things, and keep your shift's cost in line with the budget." What? This made no sense to Jake. Someone had always come alongside him and trained him. But now, the sawmill foreman was being promoted to another position, so no one would be on shift with him to show him the ropes. Now, he knew why he had felt fear earlier. His intuition told him to prepare to be fully immersed into the fire pit of a management position.

Having spent a few years being a union member, Jake hadn't expected the push back that awaited him. The crew resented his being one of them on Friday, and on Monday, he became their new boss. For Jake, it meant enforcing all the rules and policies along with all other responsibilities. Where he had gathered with them in the past to smoke and drink, now he was obligated to stop the behavior.

On holiday nights in the past, each person who drank had a liquor bottle at his workstation. Workers smoked regardless of the policy. As a smoker, Jake had broken the no-smoking rule for years without any regrets. Now, he was being held to a higher standard. It seemed strange to call out the rule breakers and worse to write them up when they continued to violate the rules. After firing his first employee for breaking the rules repeatedly, an old-timer no less, the crew finally realized Jake was serious about being a foreman with integrity. He quit smoking because of his internal commitment to be an example to others.

Within three years, Jake became superintendent over the entire, multi-million-dollar facility. Jake was responsible for nine supervisors and three other superintendents, plus some 500 employees. He reported only to the plant manager. One of his first challenges was the modernization of the sawmill.

The company had planned the project for a couple of years with a budget of $7 million. The company's objective was to rebuild with new equipment to increase production and gain more recovery from each log processed. One day, the plant manager called him into his office and said, "This is your project now. Don't lose production levels, and you have three months to complete the project." Again, what? Jake wasn't an engineer and had never been responsible for such a challenge. He had no idea who to talk to or where to begin.

The only thing Jake could think to do was to call all the foremen together and let them know what was going to take place over the next three months. There was excitement and concern. Excitement because it had been decades since any new equipment had been installed and concern over what it meant for them. Would they be responsible for even more? In the end, they finished the project on time and under budget. But the greatest accomplishment was they had to remove the roof of the building for two weeks during what historically had been some of the wettest seasons of the year, and not a drop of rain fell. Jake had to give credit to the construction superintendent, Vern, as he picked the two weeks for removing the roof. It seemed Vern trusted the *Old Farmer's Almanac* when there were construction projects of such magnitude.

The project's success created within Jake such a high level of confidence that he knew he could handle whatever was entrusted to him going forward. Over the years, in the same facility, Jake modernized many more times, including installing a 12-Megawatt generator that would provide power to the plant. The excess could be fed back into the power grid and sold to the local public utility. It was an amazing project to take on, as it required a complete rebuild of the boiler system to create the super-heated steam needed to run the generator, as well as provide steam to the dry lumber kilns. To do this, the company hired an experienced project manager who oversaw every aspect of the project. Otto was a hard man to be in a relationship with, but he knew what needed to be accomplished, so everyone bit their tongues and followed his lead for the greater good. The project was completed but well after launch time and over budget. Otto took the heat and was released after the company completed the project. Everyone felt relief not having him nitpick every decision about plant improvement projects.

As the years passed, Jake took on more and more responsibility, along with the authority required to do the job. He was asked to manage another facility in Oregon while keeping his duties in his current position. Once again, Jake said yes and spent days at both facilities where he promoted two individuals to oversee the operations while he was at one of the other facilities. Things seemed to be working out when a notice was received saying the parent company out of California would be selling off all its wood products and paper holdings. That meant five sawmills, a clad-wood plant, and two paper mills would be sold or shut down. The shock of this news shot through the communities like little atomic explosions. All facilities together employed about 1,500 people. Their families and those in the small Oregon communities were going to suffer in ways they hadn't before. As a union company, the only strikes had been at the paper mills, so the sawmill and clad-wood employees had never experienced being put out on the street without a paycheck, including Jake's family. Everyone was scared to face what was inevitable.

Shortly after the announcement, the vice president of operations called Jake into his office where he was told there were a select few who would be asked to stay with the company during the sell and closing process. They would be cutting back, and some managers, superintendents, and foremen would be terminated, which meant those who would be kept on would take on more of a workload and receive a substantial stay bonus.

Joe said to him, "Jake, you are very important to this organization, and the president has authorized an offer of a stay bonus so you can keep working until the finalization of the transaction, selling off all assets of the wood products facilities and timberlands." It was an honor to be identified as a valuable employee, and of course, Jake agreed to stay. The offer included a letter from the parent company in California validating the offer. Jake would receive the letter within the coming weeks. One condition was included in the offer: Jake was not to share with anyone, including the company president, anything related to the offer. If he did, the company would withdraw the offer in full. Jake agreed, and they shook hands to seal the deal.

Weeks passed, and the letter never arrived. Jake called Joe and asked about the letter. The VP replied, "Jake, you know you can trust me, so keep doing your job, and the letter will come." Months passed without a letter coming, so he called Joe several more times, and the response was always the same: "Keep doing your job, I have your back."

The company's sale was complete, with few people noticing much of a difference in their area of responsibility except for the president, who left once the company sold. Jake retained his position as superintendent but was not convinced his position was secure with the new owners. The offer of his stay bonus seemed to vanish with the president's departure, and no one was letting him know what happened. Owning other paper mills, the Illinois company didn't seem interested in the sawmills and timberlands, which were part of the purchase. In a few months after taking ownership, they confirmed Jake's suspicions by announcing their intent to sell off the lumber and timber divisions. The industry was undergoing serious business upheaval with manufacturing plants on the west coast closing and being sold resulting from new environmental regulations that limited the supply of available timber. The uncertainty was unsettling for Jake and Grace.

During the process of his plant being sold off again, Jake was called into Joe's office and informed he had put together a team that was going to buy out a piece of the company. He said the group would like to include him. With Jake, there were a total of seven men who were working to do a leveraged buyout of the sawmills. Jake's piece of the action would include his takeover of the sawmill, where he had been the superintendent for years. The manager was moving to another location. Jake was to receive a sawmill—valued at $7 million in 1987—for being part of this group. He could not say yes fast enough. The group met a few times every week to learn the progress of the negotiations from Joe. In one meeting, Joe informed the group the parent company from Illinois wanted to be their source of capital for operations.

Jake didn't know why, but he immediately felt distrust with the idea and made it known. When the vote was cast to accept the offer or reject it, he was so convincing, that everyone voted to reject the offer. Meaning they would seek their own capital needs elsewhere, and they would not be subject to the parent company and all its decision-making processes, which had proven not to be in the group's best interest in the past. Joe delivered the group's decision to the new president. The next day, the group learned the president was so angry about their decision he sold the sawmills to another company.

Everyone in the group was devastated! They believed the company was only negotiating with them.. Everyone felt dejected, let down, and betrayed by the president. Jake thought he was more responsible than Joe as he was the one who distrusted the company and its president and lobbied the group to reject their offer. The team lost millions of potential assets. It was the first time Jake became aware of how powerful and influential he could be because of his distrust of people. To add salt to his wound, Joe and all the company's top brass left with their golden parachute without saying a word to him.

Jake was filled with rage at this development and demanded the new president pay him what was due. The new president's position was the stay bonus was on the previous company. But the president had a need. He needed Jake to manage one of the other sawmills. The door was open for Jake to negotiate a new bonus agreement, so he felt whole. With great reluctance, the president agreed to Jake's latest demand. Jake was satisfied with the money and agreed to take over the sawmill's management, even though it was away from his home.

True to their earlier announcement, the company kept the sawmills for less than a year before selling them off. Once again, Jake felt betrayed after making a sacrifice to work away from home for much of the time. But the plants were sold, and Jake needed a job.

———— ∞∞∞ ————

The company that purchased the sawmill in Jake's hometown was well known in the industry and coastal communities. They had been embroiled in breaking up their union, and the owner had made it clear he would never have another unionized plant. Jake knew the owner and had no intention of working for him because he believed he was untrustworthy. Besides, he was the one who wedged his way into negotiating the purchase of the same sawmill facilities Jake's group attempted to buy.

The sawmill had been in mothballs for months when the new owner announced an opening date. Jake had searched for a new job without success, and Grace feared they would have to move before the children finished school.

Jake's boss was hired back by the new owner and in his original position as manager. He was given the latitude to hire his management team, and Jake was his first call. He offered Jake a position with less authority and title than what Jake had under the previous two owners, but it would allow Jake and his family to remain in the community. After discussing it with Grace, Jake accepted the lower-paying position.

Jake remained with the company for five years, rebuilding the facility with more modern equipment, and once again, doubling the production. The plant manager called him in one day and informed him he was going to retire and believed Jake should take over his position. He would have to interview with the vice president of operations first. An interview was set, and Jake met with Bob, VP of operations, and went through the interview process.

Jake felt unsettled during the interview and finally asked the VP if he was in a cursory interview or a real one. Bob assured him it was real, but a few weeks later, the VP hired his friend, Eric, who Jake had interviewed with during the selling period. Eric was an arrogant dictator of a manager and thought highly of himself. Jake had interviewed with Eric at his plant during the company's sale and was relieved when Eric had decided not to offer him a position. After the interview, Jake would not take the position, even if Eric offered it to him. He could not imagine working with someone who was so overbearing and arrogant. Eric was now the new plant manager, and Jake felt his job was in jeopardy.

Three months after Eric's onboarding, he was in Jake's office demanding Jake renegotiate a purchase of a major piece of equipment for the generator's cooling tower. Eric wanted the part weeks earlier than the vendor promised. Fearing for his job, Jake agreed to contact the vendor and see what could be worked out. For Eric, that was not good enough. He wanted Jake to promise he would get the part in the time frame Eric asked for. So, Jake promised, knowing full well the vendor would not agree without substantially increasing the price, which Eric already said he would not stand for. But Jake needed to move the conversation on as he had an important question to ask Eric. His question was "How are you going to gain the loyalty of the employees?"

Eric laughed and said, "Easy, I find out who the two people are in this plant everyone depends on, and I fire them." Jake's blood turned to ice because he knew his head was on the chopping block. His previous manager was safe because he was retiring at the end of the year, so who else was Eric considering?

It was not long after Eric called Jake into his office. and along with the VP of operations, Bob, Eric informed him his position had been eliminated, and he was no longer needed. His employment was terminated immediately, and he would be escorted off the property. Jake was so upset he vomited and had to rush to the bathroom. Jake was consumed by feelings he had never experienced before. He had been hired and acknowledged by the company's owner, both verbally and financially, and now it no longer needed him! What had he done to deserve this? His work record was flawless—production had been doubled, the union had been removed and existed no longer, they were doing more with fewer employees—what caused them to make such a drastic decision? Jake was offered a severance package that included counseling to prepare him for his job search, and he was informed if he defamed the company publicly, all severance would be withdrawn. With those last words, Jake signed the documentation and left the office for the last time.

Jake learned later the VP and the new manager had also terminated his day shift sawmill foreman. James had worked in the facility long before Jake, who had promoted him to foreman years earlier. The two thought a lot alike, and Jake felt he could always count on James to implement policy and follow other decisions made above his level. Sure, he may disagree with the decision, but he executed them as though he owned the decision. Jake also gave him the opportunities to express his disagreement, but sometimes the decisions were made well above Jake's authority. It turned out they were the two who Eric had determined might threaten him in his new role.

A few months into Jake's termination, he received a call from a friend and fellow sawmill manager, Don, asking him to come to work for him. He explained his maintenance superintendent had quit suddenly, and he needed to fill the position quickly. Reluctantly, Jake agreed to help him out with the understanding he would not move his family and would only fill the position until he could find and hire a replacement for his friend. Don agreed, and Jake began the new job within days. It had been years since he had been in Don's sawmill, and he was shocked at its condition. There were structural beams rotted at the base allowing the upper manufacturing floor to sag. There was so much work needed that he immediately set a remodeling project in motion.

Six months into his work, the company's original general manager, where he had started his career, contacted Jake. He was on the phone with another person who had been the quality control manager, and they were offering him a position in their new facility in northwest Washington. Jake would become the nightshift supervisor and be paid at a rate higher than any of the positions he had ever held. It also included an incredible benefits package. Jake asked why he was being offered the job. The GM said he kept hearing Jake's name come up during their search as the only person they would recommend for the job. His quality control manager, who was with him, had said the same thing.

Jake gave his notice. He moved with his wife to one of the wettest places in northwest Washington. Not long after taking the job, he learned no one there, the manager or the superintendent, had any interest in what ideas he had. He was hired without their knowledge, and his job was to produce lumber, nothing more. So, he did, and with everything he knew, Jake and his crew out produced the day shift by thousands of board feet daily.

Jake later learned the manager and superintendent would take inventory every morning trying to catch him in over-reporting production so they could fire him. But his production numbers were real, and they could not figure out how he did it, and they weren't about to stop and inquire how. So, Jake and his crew kept doing what he knew how to do, which infuriated the superintendent. Jake worked there for five years.

One day, they had issues with a computer system making the wrong cutting solutions. Lumber was being chopped up and discarded into the chipper. Earlier, Jake had made changes to the lumber specifications and saved the changes. The superintendent called him out for causing the problem during the lunch period. Jake tried to explain he was in another area of the sawmill at the time so it was not possible he had caused the problem, but the superintendent wouldn't hear it. He kept yelling at Jake, repeatedly calling him a liar. Finally, Jake had heard enough. He stood face to face with the superintendent and told him if he called him a liar once more, he would punch him in the face.

His courage shocked the superintendent, and he stepped back. "That's it. You're fired!"

What had he done? There were not any other places he could work or wanted to work in the area. Grace worked for the state at a high-security prison, but there were no other opportunities in the area for Jake.

For weeks, Jake spiraled into depression.

Out of nowhere, Jake received a call from a general manager who wanted to interview him for a superintendent position in a new sawmill being built on the other side of the Puget Sound. He told Jake they had heard about him and were interested in having him interview because of his background and increased production.

During the interview with the company's owners, their comptroller, human resources manager, and the GM, Jake asked why they were interested in him. They said they were amid a $40 million expansion and construction of a new high production sawmill and did not want to make the mistakes other companies had made. They had been told Jake was the guy to hire to keep them out of trouble. Jake was humbled and felt amazing to learn he was known in the industry for being such a man. Jake accepted their offer and began to learn all about what the project entailed.

Not long after his hiring, he learned the GM was gunning for the head saw filer. As Jake investigated the matter, all he could learn was the GM had a strong dislike for the man and secretly hoped Jake would feel the same and fire the man soon after his hiring. The problem was the head saw filer and Jake hit it off. He worked hours far above and beyond what was expected of him. His quality control in the filing room was excellent, and his safety record of his crew was superior.

He volunteered for almost any new project and offered his assistance to other departments with previous experience. He was the kind of employee anyone would want on his or her team, and the general manager hated him.

Over Jake's five years with the company, many things surfaced that, if known by the owners, he was sure they would take swift action. Though Jake reported to the GM, he felt a loyalty to the owners and decided to clue them in. He started by asking them to stop spending money on the project. He told them how the project was going, and they would spend well over the $40 million budget. He asked them to let him fix the issues and put into production the equipment already installed but not activated before authorizing further spending.

Additionally, he told them about the vendetta the GM had for one of his managers. It seemed Jake wasn't telling them anything they hadn't already heard. They had been waiting to see what he would do when Jake learned of the history between the GM and his manager and the project management team who reported to the GM.

A meeting was set up with the GM, the owners, the comptroller, the HR manager, and Jake, and everything was exposed. To say the GM was furious with him would be an understatement. His rage spewed forth until one of the owners stopped him saying he agreed with Jake. The GM's authority was being restricted to the project team, and Jake was responsible for the sawmill production and what was being installed to increase production. Jake would report directly to one of the owners from now on.

The GM looked as though life had been drained out of him. Jake could relate to what the GM must be feeling, but he was wrong to be doing what he was doing, both with the company's money and its employees. Not long after the meeting, the GM left the company, but the project team remained on board.

Once Jake made changes in who would be overseeing the project and brought the equipment online that had already been installed but not activated, production increased to over 300,000 board feet per day. The planned production budget was 110,000 board feet per day. The almost triple production should have provided them with protection against the Canadian subsidized imports. However, within a few years, the company could not keep up with the cost of timber and import competition. Production capacity had been reached, and they were out of the capital to increase it further.

Jake was under tremendous pressure from the owners who had their banks watching every expenditure closely. Whether it would have naturally occurred or came on because of his job, Jake suffered a stroke after waking one October morning. Not knowing what was happening, he entered the plant as half his vision blacked out. Finding his supervisors, he told them he was experiencing a medical issue and explained he had temporarily lost sight in his upper left field of vision. Of course, they were concerned for him, but he thought it had passed, so he decided to wait until he could get into an optometrist later that morning.

As the hours passed, his vision was not clearing up, so he drove to the nearest optometrist, where it was suggested he needed to see a neurologist immediately. He was not having a vision problem but, rather, a vascular issue.

Because of his history of migraines, the neurologist was convinced Jake was experiencing a different kind of migraine. There was no pain, but he saw images and colors he'd never seen with previous migraines. It took hours before Jake persuaded him to schedule an MRI so that they knew for certain. The MRI detailed an area in Jake's brain that had undergone a stroke that affected his vision. It was months later when Jake learned his vision loss was permanent.

The neurologist could not identify a reason for the stroke, so Jake was referred to a cardiologist. After testing, Jake was told he had a hole in his heart. He had options, and none of them were great. Without surgery to repair the hole, he was a candidate for another stroke, which had the potential to be deadly or reduce him to a vegetative state. Or he could undergo experimental surgery to repair the hole. Jake and Grace felt the surgery was his best option, so he was scheduled for surgery four months in the future.

Following his weeks in recovery, Jake returned to work only to learn the owners had promoted the temporary manager that Jake hired during his absence. He was now Jake's boss, which didn't sit well with him. Within a couple of years, the owners were offering his facility for sale. Jake was surprised, but not shocked, as the company was bleeding losses each month, and nothing could be done to stop it. Finally, in 2000, the company was shut down, and the equipment was auctioned off. Once again, Jake found himself out of work and out of ideas of what to do next.

LOOKING BACK:

Jake didn't know what to do, because three years earlier, he had experienced a stroke and open-heart surgery the following year to fix the issue that caused the stroke. He knew he would not be a good candidate for hire. Plus, the stroke had left him with a blind spot which made working in the heavy industry more dangerous than it already was.

After experiencing a stroke at the age of 47 and open-heart surgery the next year, it became glaringly clear the industry Jake had loved was now much too dangerous for him. Looking back, Jake could see he had spiraled into a deep depression. His worth had been wrapped up in what he did in his career versus who he was. Where would he turn? What would he do? If his worth were a function of what he did, then he would end up being worthless. He shut down at the thought of never being able to do the work he loved.

As years passed, Jake wanted something more, something that would challenge him while allowing him to make a difference in the world. The kind of difference that could end up being his legacy.

Jake hadn't always felt this way. Outside of his work, he hadn't needed people in his life. After all, it was people and those relationships that caused him to suffer all his life. It started at a young age with the divorce of his parents.

Short of spending thousands of hours of intentional research, much like achieving a Ph.D. on every limiting belief and fixed mindset an individual has accepted as their own, it appears there is no way forward or out of the hell they are living. It seems the individual is captive to their position in life—from the cradle to the grave—it looks hopeless.

Jake's story reveals there is hope, and for those who are willing to do a deep dive into self-introspection, they, too, will find their fork in the road that leads to the life they were meant to live, a life of abundance, joy, peace, love, acceptance, courage, and worthiness.

At this point in Jake's life, he hasn't yet gained an understanding of why his life has evolved the way it has. His was an entanglement of chances and circumstances that came together at the right time and place, manifesting his current situation. He believed he was in control, making his own decisions.

When you examine closely, you will see some underlying limiting beliefs and decisions have been at the root of all his decisions. His deep-seated victim, scarcity, and poverty thinking drove him to take unexamined risks, with consequences Jake hadn't considered.

Feeling like he had no say or control, he gave up and slid into a dark depression. For the next two years, he would become intimate with his La-Z-Boy® chair, caring little about anything and people.

YOUR INTROSPECTIVE CHALLENGE:

1. What are some of your fixed mindsets and limiting beliefs?

   _____

   _____

   _____

   _____

2. How have these mindsets and beliefs held you back?

   _____

   _____

   _____

   _____

3. What are the prices you and others have and are paying?

   _____

   _____

   _____

   _____

4. What legacy do you hope to leave?

   _____

   _____

   _____

   _____

IV

LIFE SHOULDN'T BE THIS WAY

Once your mindset changes, everything on the outside will change along with it.

—Steve Maraboli,
Life, the Truth, and Being Free

Individuals with fixed victim, scarcity, and poverty mindsets—along with skewed worldviews—tend to believe everything and everyone is scheming against them. Subconsciously, they believe life was being *done* to them versus having any control over their life. Most are resisting their greatness while blaming everyone else for their failures. They do not understand what it means to be responsible for all their choices, so they continue to respond in the same old tired way, which generally results in disappointment and heartbreak. There comes a point in life when most adults begin to question if there is a better way of creating their hearts' desires. But the fear of putting themselves out there—taking emotional, financial, and other risks—once again, could mean if they do not get their licks in first, they may pay another huge price.

The limiting decisions, beliefs, and worldviews individuals accept as their own are lies the world wants us to believe. We believe the lies about ourselves and who we are. How relationships are supposed to work and look, how money operates on this planet, what religion is all about, how to care for our health and wellness, what love involves, how people cannot be trusted, and the other person has value. Still, I don't, and on and on. Our lies define and manifest our state of being and thus the life we create and live.

Born into a victim and poverty mindset, a bullied child grew into a man who could not find his way in relationships, business, or personal fulfillment. It was as though he was taking up space on this planet, sucking up oxygen, and killing off every relationship around him. His marriage during the Vietnam War era would become more and more like his parents' marriage. Unlike his father, he was not violent with Grace, but he projected his pain into his relationship with his wife through his booming voice, tone, negativity, and state of victimhood.

Jake had a work ethic like his mother, working double shifts and most weekends, but he lacked the skills to be in an intimate relationship with his wife as his father could not be the husband his mother needed. He was afraid he would become an alcoholic as his father had, so he resisted drinking except to fit in with the men he worked with. He could not handle alcohol well, and the less he drank, the more in control he felt. He traded being an alcoholic for a sense of control.

Jake wanted love and intimacy, but he did not possess the knowledge or skills to create it. The only way of life he knew was a difficult one. So, he poured himself into his work, which did not leave time for his family and raising his children. His marriage suffered immensely. At times, there was intense arguing, screaming, and cursing in the presence of his two children. Grace had considered divorcing him but later decided she would make the marriage work, even if she were the only one to make any effort.

Grace and Jake attended church regularly and made friends with two couples who were senior to them. Each month, they would have dinner together as part of a church project called dinner for six. The couples had a lot of fun when they were together, laughing and enjoying each other's company.

A few weeks had passed when Lucy approached Jake and Grace and asked them to attend a workshop she was hosting. Lucy was a top income earner in a multi-level marketing company, and she had invited Tom Grady to speak to her team of consultants. Grace and Jake were not part of her team, but Lucy wanted to include them anyway. Tom was going to talk about leadership. *What will that do for me?* Jake wondered.

With as much grace as he could muster, Jake politely declined Lucy's invitation. For two years, Lucy would invite this author to her team meetings to speak, each time inviting Jake and Grace to join them. She had begun to hound Jake about attending her leadership workshops, saying it would be good for him. She mentioned it when they were at church, at their dinner meetings, and when the couples were together. Of all the things she would want him to attend, leadership was not on his radar. Lucy made repeated attempts to convince Jake he needed to meet her author friend. Finally, Jake and Grace agreed to attend her next workshop. Jake felt it would be three hours of their life they would never get back, but at least they would get off Lucy's radar.

This single decision would culminate into a new trajectory for Jake's life.

The workshop was marketed as a personal growth program. Jake and Grace had never attended this kind of workshop, albeit Jake had participated in many leadership programs during his career. Jake wondered what he could possibly gain from three hours as an audience participant he had not already been exposed to over his more than thirty years in management.

But this was not your typical business workshop. It included many exercises and modules the facilitator called *experiential learning*. Jake became fully engaged, having decided if he was going to sit for three hours, then he would make the most of them.

Tom, the speaker and author, said something that hooked Jake emotionally and intellectually. It seemed Tom had figured out a way to create more value from life than Jake ever had, and he wanted more. So, at the end of the three-hour workshop, Grace and Jake signed up for a three-day program scheduled for next month.

From the first day of the seminar, Jake was experiencing so many new and revealing revelations. He did not hesitate or resist when the facilitator asked for volunteers for a new exercise. He had already learned his worldviews were the root of why he had created his life the way he had. Jake had identified he had lived from a victim mindset, which did not allow him to develop solutions for escape. He took full ownership of how his parents viewed the world and how he had integrated his parents' limiting beliefs and worldviews into his subconscious programming.

In the last exercise of day one, the participants split up into four groups, based on their answers to simple topics. Tom provided the subjects, asking the participants to identify themselves as two of four options, as either formal or informal and flow with or dominant. Tom identified the groups the participants would make up. Jake's answers put him into one of the larger groups of people. Two other groups were small with four or five people, and the fourth group was the largest of the four with a couple of dozen people.

Tom gave the instructions for this new exercise. As a group, they would answer a few questions as they applied to the group. A simple majority vote would determine if any answer was true for the group. The topics they would respond to, such as the group's likes, dislikes, whether they were buyers or sellers, task- or relationship-oriented, their strengths, and their weaknesses. Then, each group would pick a song title from all the suggestions to represent the group's overall personality and behavioral style. The groups identified a leader who would share their group's answers with the room. To complete the group's response, they would sing a verse or line of the song they had agreed represented the group.

At first, Jake's initial answers had landed him in one of the larger groups. As the group began to respond to the topics, he felt uncomfortable. This group was throwing out some bizarre answers. They liked to party and have sex, a lot of sex. They did not like aggressive or arrogant people. They identified themselves as relationship-oriented. They were split between being buyers and sellers. They were great at selling their ideas. They over-committed to people. Their song title by Queen was "We Will Rock You." All this was enough to make Jake jump from his seat, thinking this group of people were out of their minds. Who in the world could live their life believing those things? Jake began a search of the room for the group he felt was a better fit for him.

He moved from one group to the next, when finally, after listening in to the answers of the other three groups, Jake heard answers more like what he would have given. He grabbed a chair and joined a much smaller group of people.

One at a time, each group leader would stand and provide the group's answers to the topics. Jake was chosen as the leader of his group and eagerly provided their answers. With each topic, there was laughter from the other groups. Why were they laughing? His group liked to be in control, they disliked weak people, were task-oriented, were sellers, they got things done, and did not report any weaknesses. Their song choice, "I Did It My Way" by Frank Sinatra, caused the room to roar with laughter.

Jake felt embarrassed, as though the participants were laughing at him. Tom thanked the group and moved to the next group. It became clear to Jake each group was quite different from the others. One liked money and control, another liked puppies, another liked data, and Jake's original group had put sex, a lot of sex, at the top of their list. Each group's answers were vastly different from Jake's group.

Tom shared his insights about each group's answers, comparing one group's responses to another group to highlight the different behavioral and communication styles. All the groups laughed at themselves and each other. Tom continued by sharing his commentary as to why humanity struggled to be in a relationship.

Tom gave a name to each group as he finished up his talk. He named Jake's small group the controllers of the planet because they liked to control and make things happen. One other small group were analysts because they struggled to decide and act, preferring to collect more data and postpone decisions. They were easily offended and would shut down when confronted. Another group, the supporters, loved everyone and would sacrifice their own dreams to fulfill others' dreams. Though they might not like what they were doing, they would never cause problems in the relationship. The final group, the promoters, made more money than any of the other groups because they spent more. They liked to be in the limelight and were easily distracted by the next shiny object, aka squirrel opportunity, which came their way.

Jake had ended up joining the controllers and knew they were his people. He also knew why he and Grace had so many problems in their relationship. Grace seemed to have traits of two groups, the analysts and the promoters. Her work with the state required she be precise in her job. Should she make a mistake, it could result in a criminal being set free, even though they were guilty of a crime. Though she loved her job, she was always on guard to be sure she performed it precisely as the state required. But Grace was a promoter outside of her work. She loved to have fun, she was social and engaged around people, she disliked Jake's controlling style, and she started a lot of projects and struggled to finish most of them. Together, Jake and Grace would need to learn to accept each other's personalities or continue to pay high prices for resisting.

<hr />

During the three-day seminar, Tom gave instructions to a game and told everyone the object was to win, and the way to win was to accumulate the most positive points. There were two groups, with one playing their game in a different location. Each group was to select a leader, and neither group could move forward until they knew how the other group had voted and scored.

Unlike other times in his life, Jake was not selected to be the leader by the group. He had stayed behind to help a woman in a wheelchair exit the room. Once they caught up to their group, they were already playing round three. Seeing what had happened, he questioned the leader's right to be the leader and pointed out they were not allowed to play multiple rounds at a time. Stressing the only way to move forward was for each group to know how the other group voted and scored, Jake stated the way to win was evident. It was to accumulate the most positive points. The possible point matrix was listed on the score sheet, and there was only one way to accumulate the most positive points.

However, the leader would not acknowledge him. After making several attempts to make his point, the group leader pointed to Jake while yelling at the group, "Will someone shut this man up?"

Jake felt an overwhelming sense of urgency. He knew something had to be done. He had already attempted to get the group and its leader to understand the need to shift strategies, but his words fell on deaf ears. His thoughts turned to disappointing the facilitator and his friend, Lucy. She had been the runner who visited each group and shared the other group's score so both groups could move to the next frame in the game. As she approached his group again, Jake commented his group seemed to be making the wrong choices each time. Lucy looked at him with a smirk on her face. Before she could turn and walk away, Jake asked, "Couldn't we send someone to the other group and let them know our strategy so we could all be on the same page and win together?" Lucy grinned and walked away.

Confusion set in, and Jake did not understand why Lucy wouldn't answer but walked away. Wondering to himself,

Jake thought, *Why would there be any harm in sending someone to the other group, an emissary, who could share the group's strategy and get everyone on the same page?* Suddenly, a moment of clarity: *I'm someone*, he thought! It had occurred to Jake he had tried to get others to do what he was perfectly capable of doing.

In a flash, he spun around and headed for the door to the other group's room. He had gotten within about ten feet of the door when his eyes locked with one of the volunteer staff members. Mike had flown in from Toronto and was there to be of service. At this moment, he was standing between Jake and the other group. As their eyes fixated on each other, Mike shook his head ever so slightly. Quickly, Jake interpreted Mike's motion to mean there was no way Jake would be getting past him. Jake froze in his footsteps. He knew what he needed to do, but he couldn't take a step forward for some reason. What was happening, he wondered?

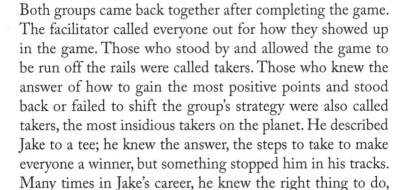

Both groups came back together after completing the game. The facilitator called everyone out for how they showed up in the game. Those who stood by and allowed the game to be run off the rails were called takers. Those who knew the answer of how to gain the most positive points and stood back or failed to shift the group's strategy were also called takers, the most insidious takers on the planet. He described Jake to a tee; he knew the answer, the steps to take to make everyone a winner, but something stopped him in his tracks. Many times in Jake's career, he knew the right thing to do, but he would acquiesce to those with more important titles or degrees. The facilitator wrapped up the game by giving homework, stressing everyone should take a full hour of silence to process their experience in the game.

Later, Jake was awakened from his slumber and sat straight up in bed. In an instant, he had seen his entire life and why his life was the way it was. He didn't trust anyone and did not know how to love himself or others. Revelation and breakthrough happened in a flash of time, and there would be no turning back. A moment of clarity had opened the door for his character transformation that came with a love for others and himself he had never felt before. Jake was experiencing clarity and the answer to why he had never trusted anyone. It was like getting hit by a bolt of lightning. He was experiencing so much pain, but it was becoming crystal clear to him he had lived in a state of victimhood, blaming everyone but himself for the life and experiences he had lived.

LOOKING BACK:

Jake had never been able to force himself to trust or feel real love for anyone. His experiences of abandonment, sexual molestation, and betrayal had left a massive hole in his heart, and he felt he dared not risk exposing himself again.

Who had he become?

As a man who settled for scraps like his parents, he wanted more, but he didn't know his value. Taking risks had been out of the question, so Jake played it safely inside his worldviews of limiting decisions, beliefs, and victimhood. Others had tried to tell him he had so much potential, but his worldviews put mistrust in others who seemed to want something from him, so he could not hear what they were saying.

Jake did not understand how different he was from everyone else. He made things happen. People jumped when he spoke. His style was overbearing and driven by fear. This was something his family knew all too well. What is wrong with a man like that? Jake thought he saw people and things as they were. He had never considered they were his mirrors. Deep depression seemed to come and stay for long periods. He could see the suffering man, himself, as though he floated above him. Jake did not know how to help him. His misery had permeated every area of his life, and those around him also paid a huge price.

Jake was 51 years old, and he had not created the kind of life he always dreamed of living. He and Grace had raised their two children, who were now on their own. They had been married for 34 years and satisfied with where they were as a couple. The rough years of their early marriage were well in the distant past. Like many other couples, they felt their good marriage had grown to the highest level of their expectations. Grace was the only income earner at the time, but now, with Jake's revelation, he was hyper-motivated to create a far better life for Grace and him than ever before.

YOUR INTROSPECTIVE CHALLENGE:

1. What are the worldly lies that have been controlling your life?

   _____

   _____

   _____

   _____

2. How does Jake's story reveal to you the opportunities you have missed?

   _____

   _____

   _____

   _____

3. What prices are you paying for not trusting others?

   _____

   _____

   _____

   _____

4. What prices are you paying for not seeing your value and loving yourself?

   _____

   _____

   _____

   _____

PART II
REVELATION

V

RISK TRUST

*You may be deceived if you trust too much, but you will
live in torment if you don't trust enough.*

—Frank Crane

W hen a person trusts, he or she will experience wounding.
But there is a much bigger price to pay when the choice is
made not to trust. The price of not trusting is the loss of
personal dreams and aspirations. Trusting is a choice everyone
will make, at times, moment by moment. The rewards of
trusting are far greater than never trusting. These might include
deeper and more intimate relationships, greater authority and
responsibility in your work-life, more opportunities, the trust
of others, recognition of your wisdom and value, respect, and
high esteem by others. Yes, from time to time, people will
betray your trust, but if you never trust, you'll never know what

opportunities you failed to notice. Possibilities live outside the boundaries people place on themselves. With small successes, those boundaries expand, exposing more of what is possible. Relationships become richer and more intimate. Business opportunities requiring a higher level of risk become easier to manage. Restoring family relations becomes a quest. And he or she will begin to attract into their life the kind of people who will bring more value and benefit than they take.

In his heightened emotional state, Jake couldn't wait to get into the seminar room the next morning. His protective guard had been shattered and had fallen away. He had a lot he wanted to say, not only to the people in the room but also to his wife. Jake had awakened Grace at 2:36 a.m., full of excitement, wanting to talk about what he was experiencing. He felt God was sharing how the world and everything that did not come from God's love would be destroyed. Instead of being terrified of such a possibility, Jake felt an overwhelming joy that seemed to have no boundaries. His heart was overflowing with, what he thought, must be God's love. For the first time he could remember, Jake felt different about himself and everyone he knew. Had he fallen in love with humanity?

Jake was the first person to speak on Sunday, the last day of the seminar. He was filled to overflowing with feelings and emotions he had never experienced. He was coming clean, publicly, about how he viewed himself and all of humanity and how his judgment of others kept him from having true friendships and business relationships. He owned his failures with Grace and his marriage, saying he had come close to running Grace off. He acknowledged that, had Grace not poured herself into the marriage, it likely would have ended in divorce many years earlier. He continued, saying he and Grace felt they had finally gotten to a place in their marriage that was good. He realized that with some shifts in his thinking, heart-level thinking, they could create a spectacular marriage. He looked at Grace, and through her tears, she nodded her head in agreement. Jake's sharing was emotional, and when he looked around the room, it seemed everyone was experiencing similar emotions. Even the facilitator had tears running down his face. *Are they grieving for me?* he wondered. Or was their story too much like his?

There was more to experience in the day, and Jake could not wait. He felt he had already gotten more than his money's worth and wanted every bit of experience he could create during the seminar's last day. The morning exercise, after the time for sharing, was what the facilitator called a dyad. People who were in a relationship with another person in the room would do the exercise together. Jake and Grace placed their chair across from one another so they were near each other.

The exercise was about giving, taking, and loving, and how each of these shows up in every relationship. The facilitator led off by asking, "What does giving look like in your relationship?" Speaking loud enough for each other to hear their answers, Jake and Grace shared their answers. Grace spoke of giving her time at church—contributing to the family income, loving him, their children, and grandchildren—and such matters. Jake was more pragmatic as he shared. He talked about giving up his dreams so he could provide for the family, how he provided protection and safety, and how he gave Grace his commitment when they first married.

They were then asked how taking was reflected in their relationship. The lights were turned down in the room, so it seemed they were the only two in the room as they answered. This question had a lot of different directions Jake and Grace could go, but they had invested a lot to be there, and this was the last day, so they decided to speak their truth. Each of them experienced powerful emotions over the next few minutes. Both had done and said very hurtful things, and both had paid huge prices. Jake said it felt good to release his energy from those wounds. Grace agreed.

Finally, the facilitator asked the question related to love and how it looks in the relationship. By this time, Jake and Grace were in full embrace, allowing their hearts to speak a truth either had not heard or felt for a long time, a truth that had been lost in the pain of their past. They loved one another deeply but had allowed deep wounding to stand in the way of their love growing. It had been more than a decade since there was openness, transparency, and honesty in their relationship, and they were making the most of those moments. For both, this module helped them create a new bonding that would become the foundation of a spectacular marriage to come.

Jake's new awareness filled his mind, but he was uncertain where to begin to create a new and better life for Grace and himself. To think everything would be different in the future seemed altruistic. He was committed to shifting his heart, so not only his family would benefit, but he, too, would begin to experience life much differently, more fulfilling.

With so much emotional release in the room, the facilitator decided to shift the energy and posed a game he called the nine dots. He drew an example: three dots across and three rows of dots. He explained the object was to connect all nine dots using four straight lines and not going through any dot twice and not lifting the writing instrument off the page. *A simple exercise,* Jake mused.

The facilitator did not give the participants long before asking if someone had come up with an answer. Jake had not completed his answer, but he felt the only solution was to work outside the boundaries of the dots.

One of the participants said she had a solution. She was invited to draw her solution for everyone to see. Like Jake, she had decided to work beyond the dots and drew an arrowhead image. The facilitator acknowledged she had a correct answer. Then, he asked them all, "Where are you looking for your answers?"

Most of the participants had viewed the dot's boundaries as though there was a box where the dots existed. The facilitator lectured the participants on their limiting thinking and challenged them to do the exercise using only three straight lines. *How is that possible?* Jake wondered. He put his mind to creating a solution much as he had done in business. Within moments, the answer came to Jake, and he drew it out on his paper. He was impressed with his rapid response until the facilitator said, "If you've solved it with three lines, do it with two, and when you solve it, do it with one line."

One line?

"Who has ever solved this problem with one line?" Jake asked. The facilitator did not respond directly to his question but, rather, said, "To solve such a problem, you can no longer think as you always have." The solution existed beyond limiting beliefs and worldviews, and it was, in fact, possible.

No one would solve the problem of either a two-line or a single-line solution before the day was over, but Jake knew he could use this challenge when he was stuck. He had often come up against major challenges in his previous career when it would take weeks or months to arrive at a solution. Now, he would draw out the nine dots and work his way from connecting all the dots with four straight lines to connect them with one line. He was sure if he could solve the latter, he could solve any challenge that came his way. Being new to this way of thinking, Jake was clueless about what lay ahead, but he was filled with excitement and curiosity. He would soon find out his newfound awareness did not seem like the prize he thought he had won.

At the end of the day, almost every participant in the seminar approached Jake and expressed their appreciation for Jake's openness and vulnerability, saying he had told their story as though Jake had lived it.

<hr />

LOOKING BACK:

Jake was feeling as though a fire was raging inside of him. Not a consuming fire, but rather, a fire that gave him energy, drive, and a renewed passion for life. Lucy and her husband could not believe the transformation Jake had gone through in only a few days. He was not the same man they had met a few years earlier. Jake was alive and wanted to share his awakening with everyone he could.

Grace and Jake met with Lucy and shared they wanted to help her spread the work she had begun. Lucy was overjoyed to have them join her, and they began to host seminars in the community. For three years, Lucy and her husband, Don, along with Grace and Jake, would host dozens of seminars. Tom, who owned the seminar company, provided several different facilitators. Together, the four of them worked hard at persuading their friends and family to attend an evening workshop.

Jake remembered how his friend, Lucy, had been so persistent with their invitation. During one of their dinner for six outings, Jake asked Lucy what had caused her to be so driven to get him into one of her workshops. With a broad smile, Lucy said, "I saw greatness you hadn't seen in yourself. I couldn't, in good conscience, ignore what God had put on my heart, which was to get you into one of the workshops so you might know and see what I and others see in you."

Jake knew Lucy cared deeply for him. Over two years, she had refused to give up on him. He had become her mission. She would not fail at completing it. He now knew he had to be the same way with his friends and family. For them to have an opportunity to create more for themselves, they, too, must come to grips with their self-imposed limitations, whatever they were. To accomplish what Jake began to believe to be his mission, he would have to overcome even more of his self-imposed limits.

He had not realized it until this moment, but he was sensitive to what others thought and believed about him. He thought he was a man of integrity, and he wanted everyone who crossed his path to believe that about him. Would people trust him enough to give up three hours of their life to hear what a stranger might say that could alter the trajectory of their life, as Jake had? How could he convey his desire for them to have the kind of revelations and breakthroughs he had? Everyone he knew had years of experience of how he had been showing up. They were going to think he had lost his mind if he said he was a different man. The only way to convince them was to reflect to the world he was a different man. He had to become maniacal about being transformed. To show up as transformed, with a different outlook, on purpose, and committed to supporting others with what they wanted to create.

The seminar had opened Jake's heart, and he loved all he was feeling and experiencing. For the first time in his life, Jake knew what he wanted, and the seminar facilitator had presented a way to claim his dreams. Grace and Jake discussed the facilitator's offer to sign up for the next, higher-level seminar, a weeklong seminar that would take place in San Francisco, California, next month. The next seminar was, what the facilitator called, a breakthrough seminar.

It didn't matter to Jake he had experienced tremendous breakthroughs in the last seminar. He wanted more. If nothing else, he would go only to celebrate what he had already gained. The tuition was expensive, but Jake knew this was a risk he had to take if he was going to become a different man, a man in charge of his destiny and not a victim to circumstances. Grace agreed, and they signed the contract and provided their payment. Soon, they would be off to San Francisco and experiencing more revelations and breakthroughs.

YOUR INTROSPECTIVE CHALLENGE:

1. What are you passionate about that causes you to feel alive?

   _____

   _____

   _____

   _____

2. What significant emotional events have caused you to shield and harden your heart?

   _____

   _____

   _____

   _____

3. How has your monumental, life-altering experience kept you from being all you could become?

   _____

   _____

   _____

   _____

4. Who does the person have to be before you choose to trust them?

   _____

   _____

   _____

   _____

VI

A GREAT AWAKENING— TAKE A STAND

What is necessary to change a person is to change his awareness of himself.

—Abraham Maslow

I f you live long enough, life, or maybe God, has a way of allowing you to cross paths with the right circumstances at the right time in your life. For some, it's hitting rock bottom after decades of addiction. For others, it's losing the love of their life. Others are shaken to their core with the loss of a friend, coworker, employee, parent, or grandparent or experiencing one's fragile mortality. When one or more of these experiences come our way, we tend to take stock of where we are in life and wonder if we missed the boat to our paradise. It seems there are two questions humans ask of themselves at times like this: Who am I, and what is my purpose on this planet?

People unwittingly adopt many of their parent's behaviors, worldviews, and personality traits. A father's tone and language to come across as confident. A mother's controlling spirit to feel safe. They become victims of these traits without ever realizing their full effects. They experience life as it's happening to them, instead of being responsible for creating value in their life. Many people never take a stand for anything because they are a victim of everything. Transforming their unconscious, victim programming can transform their unconscious and produce the kinds of results they long for and see in others.

During his career in the lumber industry, Jake underwent two monumental, life-altering, significant emotional experiences. In both cases, two of his employees' lives came to an end because of industrial accidents. He knew them both and took their deaths hard. Each time, he met with the families to let them know of the accident. In one case, the individual had died in the plant while his wife waited for him in the parking lot.

It had been years since Jake had thought about these employees and the tragic ending of their lives. He carried a pain inside he could not deal with, so he pushed it down and prayed it would go away. From time to time, the memories would come flooding back as they had during the weekend seminar. The death of these two men had awakened compassion in his heart that wasn't there before, and he didn't know what to do with it. So, like the pain, he avoided feeling it and became more hardened and guarded.

He had hired a young man who was fresh out of high school and without previous industrial employment history. Stan reminded Jake of himself when he was that age, full of energy and a willingness to take on anything to prove himself. He was hired to fill a swing-shift position, filling railroad cars with wood chips blown from the sawmill through a high-pressure pneumatic system. As a railcar was filled, it moved to a holding area, and another would be rolled into position. The railcars' tracks had a slight slope that ran through the plant, so moving one required the brake's release and the use of a wheel jack to get it rolling. Once the railcar reached the holding area, the operator applied the brakes by standing on the access steps and turning the brake wheel until the car stopped.

Though the local wood products union represented the plant employees, he could hire Stan without having to post the position for bid. There was not any incentive for day-shift employees to go on nights for a nearly entry-level position; besides, the position was out in the weather in the Pacific Northwest.

The outgoing employee would be responsible for training Stan. He was eager to help him learn all the tricks of the job because it meant he could retire as planned. Stan was a smart and efficient learner. He quickly picked up the job, and both he and his trainer felt after two weeks of on-the-job experience, he was ready to take full responsibility for the job. The supervisor talked with Jake about how quickly Stan had progressed and requested permission to award the position to him. Because of an uneasy feeling not clear to Jake, he wanted to hear from both Stan and his trainer before he gave his approval.

All four parties met the next day to discuss promoting Stan and retiring his trainer. As Jake expected, the trainer felt he had done all he could to prepare Stan for the job. He had high praise for his quickness to understand the position and importance of the operation. The position could shut down the entire sawmill operation should the job requirements not be fulfilled completely. The room for error was limited, but he felt his training had adequately addressed the issue.

Jake looked at Stan and asked, "Do you feel you have fully grasped the duties and importance of this job?"

His response was emphatic. "Yes, I do."

Not entirely convinced, he turned to the supervisor and asked, "Are you certain the training requirements have been met, and Stan is ready to be on his own in the job?"

The supervisor had over thirty years with the company and knew every aspect and expectation of the sawmill production line. Without hesitation, he said, "Yes, I know he is ready."

Jake sat back in his chair, taking some deep breaths before he delivered his message. "Okay, Stan, you have worked hard to learn the job requirements, and from what these two men are telling me, you are ready to be on your own. It is an important position in the plant, so I am counting on you to do the job, and it is on your supervisor to assure you don't fail." Turning back to the supervisor, he asked, "Are you certain of your decision to promote Stan?"

Again, without hesitation, he declared, "Yes, I'm certain."

Expecting none of the parties were going to offer anything more, Jake said, "Let's make the promotion effective tonight. Stan, you will be on your own, and your supervisor will be accountable for your production results."

For the next month, Stan performed his job duties without incident. At the same time, Jake was busy overseeing a swing-shift construction crew that included several trades, including electricians, millwrights, welders, carpenters, and vendors as they worked on one of the modernization projects in the sawmill.

A call came over his radio: "Boiler to Unit 7, Boiler to Unit 7!"

The person making the call sounded out of breath and in a panic. Jake responded, "Unit 7, go ahead."

"You're needed in the oil shack immediately!"

It wasn't enough information, so he asked, "What's going on in the oil shack?"

"It's Stan, and he's been hurt really bad!"

His worst fears had come to pass concerning this new young man. Something had happened, and he was being summoned to assist. Making his way to the oil shack, a small building filled with barrels of lubricants for the heavy equipment used at the boiler fuel pile, he saw Stan and Glenn, the operator of the International crawler used to push fuel into the feeder that kept the boiler furnace burning.

"What's happened to him, Glenn?" he asked.

"I don't know, but he can't talk, and he has been moaning and holding his stomach since I found him."

Jake noted Stan's coloring was grayish, but he wasn't bleeding anywhere. "Stay with him, and I'll call the ambulance." Darting out of the building, he called out to the first person he saw and instructed him to remain there and direct the ambulance to the oil shack. Making his way to his office, he called for the ambulance and quickly returned.

Stan seemed to be in greater pain, and Glenn needed to get back and push up more fuel for the boiler, or the fire would go out, and the boiler would go down. Kneeling beside Stan, Jake asked him what had happened. He still couldn't breathe well and couldn't speak at all. Taking off his winter jacket, he wrapped Stan to keep him warm. Lying down beside him, he placed his arm under Stan's head and comforted him as best he could.

It didn't take long for the ambulance to arrive. Jake saw the flashing lights flickering off the boiler building and heard the siren. Moments later, two EMTs entered the small building. Instantly, Jake noticed the look on the first EMT's face. His eyes seemed to bulge out of their sockets. *What does he see that I didn't?* he silently wondered.

Setting his equipment down, the EMT asked, "What happened to this man?"

Jake didn't have any good information at the time and could only respond, "We don't know yet!"

Both EMTs seemed to have a heightened level of concern and began to care for Stan with great urgency. "Find out what happened, and we'll get him to the hospital," said one of the EMTs. Immediately, Jake ran out to find Glenn, who had called him on the short-wave radio.

Glenn was finishing up with a fresh load of fuel for the boiler and was walking toward Jake. "What the hell happened, Glenn?" Jake barked out.

"I don't know," he said. "Stan came over to the fuel pile and said he couldn't get the loaded railcar to move and wanted me to give it a push with the crawler before the sawmill had to shut down, or the blowpipe became plugged with chips."

"Did you push the car for him?"

"I didn't want to at first, but he was insistent, saying if the mill went down, he might get fired, so, yes, I did."

"Then, what happened?"

"I took the crawler back to the fuel pile, because with a slight push, the car began to roll."

"Did you see where Stan was?"

"Not until I parked the crawler and went to check on him to make sure the car hadn't stalled out on the track."

"Where was he?" Jake was getting impatient with Glenn's long, drawn-out explanation of the events.

"I saw him staggering out from the back end of the rail car I had pushed. He looked like he was in pain and came into the oil shack and lay down on the floor. That's when I called you."

It wasn't a lot of information, but the ambulance was gone, and he could at least get to the hospital and let them know what he had learned. Stan was in emergency surgery by the time he arrived, so the best he could do was deliver the information to be passed on. He wanted to know what had happened and why Stan was gray when he found him.

The only person right now who could shed any light on the matter was the surgeon, so he decided to wait for him to come to the waiting room. Stan's parents had arrived, and they, too, were waiting to hear more about Stan's condition.

Hours passed while everyone's attention was fixed on the other end of the hallway where surgery was taking place. The large double doors opened, and a lone man dressed in green scrubs approached them. He was the surgeon. He explained whatever had happened to Stan, he had suffered a devastating blow to his abdomen. There was nothing they could do for him as his liver was destroyed. Stan had died on the operating table.

Jake didn't want to believe what he was hearing. Only six weeks ago, he had interviewed and hired this young man. And 30 days ago, he expressed his confidence in his abilities to do the job on his own. What had happened that was so traumatic this young man had died on his watch? He had to find out and find out quickly.

Stan's parents sobbed uncontrollably, but he had to get back to the plant and investigate the accident before everyone went home for the night. Expressing his condolences and promising he'd get the answers they all wanted, he excused himself.

The first thing he did was call his boss, Jerry, and let him know of the accident. No one had died from a plant accident to his knowledge. What was the protocol? Who had to be notified? It was late in the swing shift, but his boss answered the phone.

Quickly, Jake gave an overview of what he knew, ending with, "I need to get to the bottom of this before the shift ends, and people leave." Jerry told him not to call anyone else. He'd take care of it so he could begin investigating.

Jake quickly made his way to the boiler, where the graveyard crew was already taking over. Both the boiler operator and Glenn were still there, so he took them aside and began to question them. No one had anything more to add than what he already knew, so he sent the two of them home. Jerry and the human resource manager arrived and wanted to see where the accident happened. The three of them walked out along the rail line as Jake reviewed what he knew. Standing where the railcar would have been parked while being loaded, they looked over the surrounding area. As Glenn had explained, they could see the crawler's tracks where he had pushed the railcar. The fully loaded railcar was still parked where Stan had been seen staggering from the back end of it. A log bulkhead had been erected only a few feet from the railcar's position to stop any runaway railcar inside the plant. The rail tracks went through the plant and across a busy road close to the high school. A runaway rail car was a danger to the public, so Jerry had ordered the bulkhead to be built some years earlier.

They began to inspect every inch of the bulkhead where the railcar might have impacted with flashlights in hand. Scarring between two of the logs was found, as was wood fiber on the railcar's connection coupling. But there wasn't a hole in the logs, and the rail car was at least four feet away from the bulkhead. Climbing up the ladder at the end of the railcar, Jake called out that the brakes were fully set. Nothing was making sense. *How had Stan been hurt so badly?* they wondered out loud.

Nothing more could be learned in the dark. The swing shift crew had gone home, and the project crew had finished for the night. The boiler was at full steam, and its graveyard crew had things under control. Jerry told Jake a state investigator would be on-site in the morning, so they agreed to go home and get some rest. The next day would likely be a long one.

Jake wouldn't get any sleep as he replayed over in his thoughts every conversation and interaction he had ever had with Stan. He liked him from their first meeting when Jake interviewed him. Stan was eager and energetic and, for an 18-year-old, he seemed to have a good outlook for what he wanted and what he was willing to do to attain his goals.

Jake decided to approve of him being promoted to the job, and he was released to perform the job on his own. Was there something in the training they had missed conveying, or had Stan taken matters into his hands and acted outside of the safety of the job description? Having the crawler operator push the railcar was not part of his training or standard operations.

Glenn had been around for over 30 years, so he should have known better. They had access to the millwrights, and there were other ways to get a railcar moving. Why had they decided to do what they had? His mind raced with questions and scenarios.

Jerry and Jake were at the plant before sunrise. There was more to learn, and they wanted to get as much information as they could while protecting the accident site before the state's investigator arrived. The human resources manager would wait for the investigator and bring them to the site as soon as possible. Jerry had called several people: the president of the company, the vice president, the general manager, and the vice president of HR. By the time the investigator arrived, the VP of HR had already met with his HR manager.

The decision was made to keep the sawmill shut down during the investigation. Otherwise, the railcar would need to be removed, and that would not be acceptable to the state investigator. Jerry and Jake had enough time before the two from HR and the investigator arrived on the scene to learn about the probable sequence of events from the night before. They learned from the boiler graveyard crew Glenn had returned and told them more than what he had told Jake.

The crew reported Glenn had pushed the car, but it rolled too fast. Their theory was Stan had released too much of the brakes when he couldn't get the railcar moving with the rail jack. Then, after Glenn had pushed the car and it was rolling too fast, Stan ran to the brake wheel end of the railcar and tried to stop it before it hit the log bulkhead. Glenn had heard the impact, and when he went to check, he saw Stan stumbling from the end of the car.

Upon closer inspection, Jerry and Jake had concluded the railcar had impacted the log bulkhead with the car-to-car coupling going between two logs. It appeared the railcar had hit with full force and bounced back to the location where they found it the night before. It was obvious Stan had set the brake fully, but the railcar's speed, with its full load of wood chips, overpowered the brakes. The bulkhead was the only thing standing in its way. Stan was on the steps to the brake wheel when the railcar impacted the bulkhead and was caught in between the end of the railcar and the bulkhead. They concluded Stan had continued trying to stop the railcar with the brakes fully set by turning the brake wheel to its maximum. He either didn't have time to jump off or didn't notice how quickly the railcar was approaching the bulkhead.

The state investigator did his job thoroughly. He didn't conclude anything more had happened than what was already known and concluded from the evidence. He did interview both swing and graveyard shift boiler crews and Jake. He determined the company's training met the state's standards, and there would not be any charges brought against the company or any of its management. It was all good news to hear, but it wouldn't bring Stan back, and his family would feel the pain of their loss for the rest of their lives. Jake wasn't sure he could forgive himself for his decision to promote Stan so quickly, regardless of the state's conclusion.

Stan was the first man who lost his life during Jake's tenure as plant superintendent. Bob, one of the construction crew millwrights, was killed when he lost consciousness and fell into a conveyor that distributed fuel into the boiler ovens. He was called in during graveyard shift by the boiler crew and left alone to observe and determine the best course of repairs to make. When the boiler operator returned where he left Bob, he was nowhere to be found. After an unsuccessful search, he called Jake and told him the boiler was being shut down due to lack of fuel, resulting from the breakdown of the conveyor. He learned Bob's wife had driven him to the plant, so Jake went to the parking lot and found her alone. She hadn't seen Bob since arriving, so Jake rushed back to the boiler.

Fearing the worst had happened, Jake called the fire department and asked for a rescue team to come and help search for Bob. A short time passed, and Bob was found entangled in the distribution conveyor. The medical examiner said Bob had died almost instantly when he fell.

It was another gut punch so painful for Jake he vowed to take matters to the company's highest level and demand support for making changes in the entire company. He was done with the union protecting the employees who were committing unsafe acts and causing injury to others or themselves. In all his time at the plant, not one management person had taken the kind of stand for employee safety he was going to take.

To his surprise, Jerry said he would back whatever he wanted to do about the issue, including placing a call to the president of the company to set up a meeting for Jake to lay out his plan. Meeting with all the supervisors to explain his plan of action was his first step. They either had to buy in or look for work elsewhere. They had covered their employee's minor safety violations to make their departments' safety record look good for too long. Most of them had been with the company for more than 20 years, so quitting wasn't an option any of them wanted to consider.

Next, he met with the union job stewards who worked throughout the plant. Some of them pushed back, believing the company wasn't doing enough to protect them from the dangers of the jobs. Jake promised he would get the necessary approval and, with their help, identify those dangers and cure them.

Finally, he met with the union business secretary. He, too, worked in the plant and was aware of what Jake had been up to. There was no way he would let the company come down on his people for safety violations that had been overlooked and accepted for decades. Jake knew he had to stay cool, or he would lose his advantage in the conversation.

"Art, I completely agree our supervisors have dropped the ball by looking the other way for minor safety violations. Hell, I remember when I was a new hourly employee and worked alongside you in the plant. We did things to cut corners we knew were unsafe. And all that and every other safety violation have led to the deaths of two men. Frankly, Art, I don't want to work here another minute if we can't do more to protect our people. You have a responsibility for their safety as the union business secretary, and we have a responsibility as the employer. You can either stand with me to eliminate accidents or not. We are going to change the way we approach safety and prevent any more deaths."

What could Art say? He didn't want the word to get out he didn't care what happened to his people. Their union dues paid his salary. His role was to stand in for his people, not to be an opponent in a battle, but he always came loaded like hunting a bear. Standing up, he reached out to shake Jake's hand. It was as though he was setting his ego and pride aside as he agreed to support the company's effort to reduce accidents overall. This was a huge accomplishment and would go a long way in laying out his plan with the company president.

A corporate meeting was called, and Jerry and Jake were asked to present their plan for improving safety in the company. Jake knew unless there were significant changes throughout the company, his plan would not have the strength it needed to succeed. The president announced to all the managers and corporate staff members Jerry and Jake would be presenting a new company safety plan to address reducing plant accidents throughout the five sawmills, two paper mills, and the Cladwood plant.

Jake was caught completely by surprise, as he was familiar with the sawmill operations but not the other plants. The paper mills were the pride of the California parent company, so what were the managers going to think when Jake's plan was implemented, and they had to fall in line? He wasn't expecting his plan to impact all 1,200 employees in the company.

He relished his accomplishments.

LOOKING BACK:

Other than his employees, Jake hadn't made any kind of presentation to his peers before. He knew this moment in time was, for him, a defining moment. He would persuade the top leaders in the company that the accepted unsafe practices had to be over and done to prevent more men and women employees from being injured and possibly dying on the job.

He accepted full responsibility for allowing minor unsafe practices to lead to the deaths of his two employees. If the president was to fire him after his presentation, he was prepared. The mindset that production was more important than people had to change throughout the company, and Jake's mindset was already quite different from the one he had when he interviewed Stan. Facing family members and telling them their husband, wife, son, or daughter would never return from work was something he prayed he'd never have to do again. He was feeling a connection to his employees he hadn't before. Titles, positions, and authority had not stopped Jake this time; he took a stand for his company and its employees.

Over the next three years, his supervisors and employees, under his leadership, identified and corrected hundreds of items that had the potential to cause injury. A new normal was created where the employees began to watch out for each other. Mindsets had shifted, resulting in over one million man-hours worked in his plant before an accident requiring more than first aid occurred. This was an unmatched accomplishment in the industry, and Jake believed the deaths of Stan and Bob were the bedrock that led to his mindset awakening.

YOUR INTROSPECTIVE CHALLENGE:

1. What have you done to "take a stand" for your beliefs and principles?

   _____

   _____

   _____

   _____

2. What were the results of the stand you took?

   _____

   _____

   _____

   _____

3. What significant emotional event have you experienced that has caused you to shift your thinking and take a stand for others?

   _____

   _____

   _____

   _____

4. What are the prices you and others have paid for your casual approach to your life and career?

   _____

   _____

   _____

   _____

VII

AWARENESS SUCKS

Who looks outside, dreams. Who looks inside, awakens.

—Carl Jung

Many have no idea what they want from life because they have been in hiding for so long. Often, no one in their family knows of the secrets and significant emotional events they suffer from, such as sexual molestation, addiction, financial ruin, betrayal, job losses, childhood trauma, and spousal abuse. They may not be aware of their abandonment issues and how it was foundational in forming their programs and beliefs with trust. They fall into the trap of allowing life to happen to them instead of taking control and creating their full potential for a fulfilling life. Could they possibly transform their unconscious programming so they can also produce the kinds of desirable results they see all around them?

———— ∝◈◈∽ ————

Following the loss of his last job, his La-Z-Boy chair consumed Jake's time. He was taking up space and sucking up oxygen. He had no drive and no desire for anything. He often wondered, *Is there another way to create and live my life?*

Victimhood had become a way of life for him. He judged everyone and everything from his limiting beliefs and skewed worldviews. To Jake, people were objects or obstacles he had to control or overcome to get the desired results. How was it possible he had lived his whole life this way? The pain he was experiencing hit him with overwhelming force. Jake experienced an awakening, a revelation he had demanded unconditional trust to be in a relationship, but he refused to trust anyone, at any level. *"What an arrogant S.O.B you have become,"* he said to himself.

Should I expose my heart and trust and risk getting hurt again? he wondered. He had been living with so much pain in his life. He thought it couldn't get any worse; he decided it was worth a try. The revelation around not trusting had opened Jake's mind up to such an extent he could see possibilities in every area of his life, where he hadn't been able to see them before.

Finally, for the first time, he saw other people as human beings. They were exactly like him. Like Jake, they had pain—sorrows, fears, wants, wounds—and wanted so many of the same things he wanted. He had been resisting his heart's desires his entire life. And a new insight emerged within him. Now, he not only could feel his emotions, but he also wanted to feel the full depth of his feelings. For the first time, he could see how he had taken on his parents wounding as his own and how he had passed the same onto his children. He could turn all of it around by using his childhood trauma as fuel to move forward. Jake's Game of Life experience had broken down his guard so he could see his victim and scarcity mindsets, as well as his judging worldviews.

What if he owned all his results versus blaming others for them? What if he took responsibility for everything? He would respond differently to his circumstances and show up responsible for them. All it would take from Jake would be to be fully committed to the results he wanted to create. Jake felt freedom from heartbreaking pain he had never felt. A simple choice to respond differently had set him free. By releasing the anchors of his childhood trauma, his inner child would no longer control his destiny.

It was April 2002; the month Jake and Grace would fly to San Francisco to attend the advanced-level seminar. Jake's passion for his new life had driven him forward, and he couldn't wait for this next seminar. By engaging in every aspect of the workshop, he would create maximum value for himself and his family. *But what will that look like?* he wondered. Lucy and Don had already attended the seminar months earlier, and they weren't sharing anything not to contaminate Jake and Grace's experiences. The month of April would be filled with many events, including Jake's mother's passing only two weeks before his flight to San Francisco.

The call came from his brother, Noel, telling him their mother had died. She lived with his brother on his property in a small trailer house Noel had set up for her. Bertha had lived her entire life with minimal possessions or money. She died a Christian, and during previous visits, Jake learned she was looking forward to leaving this earth to go to her heavenly home. Bertha had never reconciled with her husband, living more than 40 years in solitude. The news of her death hit Jake hard.

It must be a test! he thought.

He felt he was being tested on his commitment to transform his character, which included attending the next seminar. His commitment was under assault. He asked himself, "How am I going to deal with this test?" His brother asked him to come back and help dispose of their mother's possessions, which was bad timing for him with the seminar on his mind and the horizon. He felt conflicted between what his brother was asking and his commitment to himself to keep growing. It was time to put what he had learned from the earlier seminar to work and create more of what he wanted. After all, he could figure out a way to do both.

As his mother had been giving away all her possessions for some time, there wasn't much to distribute. She always gave to the point there was little left for her. Jake thought of his last visit in the spring of the previous year when she wore seven blouses to stay warm. She hadn't purchased anything new for decades, and her clothes were so threadbare from being laundered. It took many layers to provide comfort.

Boxes of material strips Bertha had collected for quilting were piled up on the front porch. She and her sisters had quilted together for years, but her hands had become so arthritic she couldn't work with the frames or do the needlework any longer. Bertha must have spent years collecting all these strips of material, and now they would be burned in a pile of debris.

As he and Noel worked their way through the house, Jake found neatly wrapped bundles of letters. These letters were from the era of the Second World War and were written by his father. *Why would my mother have kept these letters for so many decades after divorcing my father?* he wondered.

As Jake held the bundles of letters in his hand, a memory popped up in his mind he couldn't set aside and ignore. His father was back home after being gone for several months. He and his mother were fighting and, at times, hitting each other.

Bertha shouted at his father, "You're crazy! Whatever happened in the war made you crazy."

Jake remembered those words exactly as they had been spoken. His father had looked at Bertha with a scowl and responded, "You're the crazy one. I'll prove it to you."

The next week, Jake's father admitted himself to Patton Mental Hospital in San Diego for psychiatric care. He would be there for several weeks of observation and treatment. Jake was far too young to understand what all of it meant. His mother told the kids their father was sick in his head and would be in the hospital for a while.

Weeks passed with his father gone, but this time, it was different because his mother seemed to look forward to bringing him home. The hospital called and informed Bertha they were releasing her husband the following day. The day had finally arrived, and Bertha gathered the kids together, telling them they would go and pick up their father. He was being released from the hospital and coming home.

Jake's older sister asked her what the doctors found out. His mother responded, "Well, he's not crazy according to the doctors, unless he's crazy like a fox, but he seems to love seeing others in pain."

One of Jake's last memories of his father was when he had come back home after being away for months and was trying to convince Bertha to take him back. In the kitchen, Jake was washing up the breakfast dishes, and he could hear every word spoken between them. Bertha was in no mood to listen to his father's explanation or excuses for leaving. She knew all too well his alcoholism was behind every decision he made. They argued for what seemed like hours before his father blurted out, "You and those damn kids have been a ball and chain around my neck our entire marriage!"

Bertha stepped back, took a breath, and as calmly as she could, said, "Listen to that."

Confused, his father shot back, "Listen to what?"

Then, the last words Jake would ever hear his mother say to his father, "The sound of that damn ball and chain hitting the floor. Get out, get out, get out, and never come back."

Jake couldn't imagine the depth of hurt those words had inflicted upon her heart. For 28 years, his mother had given in to his father's demands, expectations, and his alcohol addiction. But in a moment, with a few sharp words, his father had ended it all. Jake saw his father one other time, many years later, before he died in an auto accident.

Jake was more than curious about what his father had written to his mother. He had been wounded in the last war campaign he fought in and wrote the letters from his hospital bed. Who was this man who went to war? What did he have to say to his wife? Finally, Jake couldn't resist any longer and opened one of the letters. The words he was reading were not at all what he expected. It was like he was reading a stranger's words written to his lover a lifetime ago. He opened another letter and found the same kinds of sentiments on the page. The man who wrote the words was gentle, loving, caring, and optimistic.

Bertha was pregnant with their fourth child, and his father wanted to name the baby after his nurse if it was a girl. *Was this the same man who had fathered me?* he wondered. If it was, Jake never knew him. The father he knew was mean, hateful, and seemed to love to see people hurting.

"Enough of this letter reading," Jake said aloud, which caused his brother to ask him what he was doing.

As Jake started to explain, his brother shot back at him, "Burn those damn letters. They're both gone now, and whatever is in those letters won't make any difference."

Jake knew he was right, but it seemed there was a lot more to his father than the man he had seen come and go all those years.

The day of his mother's funeral was a hard day for Jake and his two brothers. Hank, his youngest brother, was overwhelmed with grief. Jake surmised after he had left home, Hank was left alone with his mother for more than two years before he joined the U.S. Navy. Her death ended that chapter of his life, and whatever regrets he had would never be reconciled.

Jake and Grace were excited to finally be in San Francisco where their next seminar was taking place. As they waited for the workshop to begin, a woman who sat in the lobby struck up a conversation with them. She was a former schoolteacher and married with a couple of boys. Assuming she was one of the new participants, Jake and Grace began to share their earlier experiences in the previous seminar.

Her next question was strangely worded, causing Jake to take a long pause before he answered. "What are you going to create this week?" she asked.

"Create?"

"Yes, what are each of you intending to create while you are here this week?" It was as though the two of them had not given any thought to what they might create as the previous weeks had been focused on the passing of Jake's mother.

Not knowing what their new friend was after, Jake said, "More of what we got at the last seminar."

Though his answer didn't seem to be satisfying to her, she said, "Oh, that's great."

Suddenly, the doors opened, and the people who had been on the inside of the room came out and invited everyone to enter and find a seat. There were a lot more people attending, some Jake recognized from the last seminar.

A familiar face stepped to the front of the room. It was their new friend, Donna, who had asked what they intended to create. She was one of the facilitators who would be working with them over the next five days. Donna introduced herself and acknowledged those she had met in a previous seminar, adding she was excited to get to know everyone. She introduced Tom, indicating he was the owner and would also be with them most of the week. Lastly, she introduced Dan, saying he was the lead facilitator and was here to help everyone with whatever they wanted to create.

Dan was a large man, not in physical stature but in the way he seemed to fill the space of the room. When he spoke, everyone wanted to hear what he had to say. Jake had never met a man like him and didn't quite know how to take him.

Those first three hours were filled with lectures from Tom, Dan, and Donna. Each of them had something specific they wanted to talk about. Donna was interested in what the participants were going to create throughout the week. She asked various people the question she had asked Jake and Grace in the lobby.

Dan talked about baseball. Jake had a hard time understanding what Dan was getting at until he began to talk about first base representing where people were now and second base where people said they wanted to go. But the only way to get there was to leave their baggage behind. They couldn't hang onto first base, where they were, and expect to get to second base, where their dreams and goals were.

Okay, Jake thought, *makes sense, but where are we going with this?*

Dan seemed to know what everyone was thinking and looked straight at Jake and asked, "What comes up for you when you take a risk?"

Jake could only think of one thing: the same thing had always come up for him when he put himself at risk. He answered, "Fear comes up for me."

"Yes, fear," Dan shouted. He explained, to get from first base to second base, the runner had to take the risk of being tagged out. He then seemed to strike a chord with most people in the room as he explained what most people do is try to hang on to first base while reaching for second base. He said, "Most try to drag first base with them."

Jake realized they were being lectured about hanging on to their past when, at the same time, they were trying to create a future, and the two wouldn't go together. Second base would be the goal for this week, and the only way to get there was to let go of all the baggage. How in the world was he going to let go of all the baggage he'd carried around his entire life? *Is it even possible?* he wondered.

Tom, a much smaller man, had a larger vision. Tom was about making a world that worked for everyone, and he spoke of things far beyond what Jake had ever considered for himself or even for others. *How do you create a world that works for everyone when you haven't made one that works for yourself and your family?* Jake wondered.

It seemed impossible to Jake, yet Tom seemed intent this was the organization's mission. This was something his organization was going to accomplish. He talked about all the different countries where they were working and the countries on the drawing board where they were being called to. It all seemed like such a huge vision to Jake, and he couldn't quite wrap his mind around it.

———— ∞∞ ————

Dan presented ground rules everybody had to agree with to remain in the seminar. The way to acknowledge you agreed was to stand up. Anyone who didn't stand up would have a conversation with Dan, and if he didn't like his or her point or was unwilling to modify the ground rule, he excused them from the seminar, and they left.

One ground rule was everyone needed to be on time. Dan was very explicit about what being on time looked like. Being on time meant everyone was to be in their chair with only a notebook—glasses, a glass case if needed, contact case, if needed—and a writing instrument. A jacket or sweater was permissible, but nothing else could be at the chairs. Everyone was to be seated in what Dan called open body position. People were to sit in their chairs with both feet firmly on the floor with palms resting and facing upward in their lap.

When someone shared in the room, they would stand in an open body position. They stood in front of the chair with their legs against the chair, arms at their side. If someone was moving their arms around while sharing, the rest of the people were to call them out for not following the ground rules. There was not going to be any flailing around with the arms.

After Dan gave the ground rules, everybody was dismissed for a break where they gathered in the hallways for drinks and snacks. No one really connected or talked much to one another. Jake took it more as a time to refresh and get ready for the next session. He had no idea what it was going to be about. He hadn't seen Grace for most of the morning but didn't give it a second thought. Soon, the doors opened, and everybody entered the room.

———— ∞ ————

When the doors opened, people entered the room, lackadaisically placing their belongings on a table in the back of the room and making their way to a chair.

One of the instructions was to sit in a chair so you were separated from people you knew and not to sit in the same chair twice. For Jake, he didn't care where he sat. Others were quite slow, and then suddenly, in a loud and authoritative voice, someone called out, "Doors closing now!"

Jake was startled as in a booming voice, Dan yelled, "Freeze!"

Silence descended upon the room. *Freeze? What does that mean?* Jake wondered. "Stop moving—have some integrity," Dan barked.

Those standing looked, with startled gazes, and wondered, *Is he talking to me?* Then, Dan looked at a participant straight in the eyes, calling him by name, and asked, "Why are you late?"

What an interesting question, Jake thought to himself. Why was I late? His internal dialogue spoke. We were on break and came back. How could we be late?

Dan spent several minutes one person at a time with those who remained standing, asking them why they were late. The reasons given were astounding. Some of the reasons were "I had a water bottle in my hand, and I needed to put it on the back table," or "I couldn't find an open chair," or

"There were too many people in front of me, and I didn't want to push them aside."

Dan wasn't buying their excuses. He was persistent as he continued to ask, "Why are you late?" one person after the other.

Then, finally, someone said, "I guess I wasn't committed to being on time." Dan stopped in his tracks. "Correct! It's the only answer you ever need to give. You want to know why you haven't created the results you said you wanted? There is your reason. You're not committed."

His next question caused everyone to gasp. "Where else in your life are you not committed?"

When he was working with one of the other participants, Jake answered the questions in his mind. He knew clearly he hadn't been committed to himself for decades. Had he been committed to his marriage or Grace? They had gotten to a place of having a good marriage, but he knew something was lacking. They both knew it. Were they committed to one another? Jake would process this question for a while during the week.

Then Dan said, "If you ever want to know why you don't have the life you desire, it's because you're not committed. Where else in your lives are you not committed?" The statement hit everyone like a ton of bricks at the same time.

Dan asked everyone to imagine there were sacks of money in front of the room. Inside each sack was a million dollars, and on it was the names of each person in the seminar. He continued by telling them if during the week, everyone showed up without being late, ever again, not even one second late, then at the end of the week, each person could take their sack of money home.

He asked those in attendance if it would change how they were in a relationship with each other. Would they care if a person liked them or didn't like them when they were trying to get into the room? Would it matter if there were a crowd of people in front of them? If they wanted a million dollars, to do anything they wanted, were they willing to take the step to assert themselves and be fully committed to being on time?

Everyone agreed they would as Dan challenged the room. With a smile, he said, "We'll see, we'll see."

The participants were asked to put themselves into a smaller group of people. Each group was given a poster board with several questions and statements on it. Each person was to stand in front of their group and respond to the questions and statements. The questions weren't difficult, but they were intrusive. First, each person would say their name, marital status, where he or she lived, and how many children they had.

Then came the question: "What's the negative judgment you have of yourself?" *A negative judgment?* Jake wondered. Suddenly it came to him. The negative judgment he had of himself he had said many times before was he was too controlling. Then came the question: "What's the price you pay for this negative judgment?"

Jake knew immediately. "I don't have the life of my dreams. I never have and don't know if I ever will."

Then a question that was worded so strangely it was difficult for Jake to comprehend at first. "What are the qualities you're committed to bringing out in yourself this week?"

Qualities? Why are they asking about qualities? Are they talking about virtues? Feeling confident, Jake said he was committed to being honest, transparent, and engaged.

He read the last question: "What is the price you're willing to pay this week to become the leader you're intended to be?" *What's the price I'm willing to pay? Well, I guess I'm willing to be embarrassed, which would be awful,* Jake thought. He remembered a silent childhood vow he made to himself about never allowing anyone to embarrass or humiliate him ever again. Was he willing to take that kind of risk?

The time had come to be done with his pain of the past, so yes, he would take the risk. Jake continued by saying, "I'm willing to be coached."

He felt he was coachable. He was willing to do almost anything, but Dan wouldn't let him get away with that answer, so he had to be specific. Jake was willing to put himself in embarrassing positions. He was willing to be coached, and he was willing to change his thinking. Dan responded, "Great. Take your seat."

Everyone in their groups answered their questions, after which all groups came together and received an instruction to find somebody in the room he or she would buddy up with. They would be buddied up male-to-male, female-to-female, but it had to be somebody in the room they had judged.

Jake focused on possible men he could pick. He considered two men in the room, but the man named John drew his attention. He was a small individual, clean-shaven, shaved head, but he had a rough look about him, and there was something Jake wanted to know about him.

In haste, fearing someone else would pick John, Jake acted and chose John as his buddy. Jake learned later John was the perfect choice for him. Jake and Grace had a son, Martin, who had come out to them after entering the Air Force. After disclosing he was gay, Jake didn't know what to do and stopped trying to develop a relationship with his son.

Jake had been raised in a bigoted, opinionated, and judgmental family, so when Martin came out, Jake judged him harshly. Being in the Air Force made it easy not to be in a relationship because he was gone. He was stationed in another state, making it difficult for Grace and Jake to visit him. He was trained as a medical technician and ended up being a medical trainer, but the two of them really could not find a way to connect. Jake realized John had some of the same dispositions and mannerisms as Martin and guessed he, too, was gay. Within hours, Jake's suspicions would be proven true.

John connected with Jake and disclosed he was gay. Jake thought if he could learn how to be in a relationship with a gay man, could he also learn it with his son? He felt proud of himself for picking John, but what he didn't know was the relationship would challenge him the entire week.

John and Jake would go to dinner together, and one of the tasks given during the dinner was to find out about each other, but there were some specific things Dan asked these buddy pairs to find out. The first was to learn why his buddy was there and what they wanted to create during the week. Lastly, what were the buddy's chicken exits? He explained a chicken exit is a position your buddy takes when he or she is pressed and comes up against his or her boundaries. Would he or she become angry, frustrated, or confused, or would he or she use humor to distract—and redirect?

"Everyone has them," Dan said. "Find out what your buddy's chicken exits are, because when it gets difficult this week, they will default to their dominant chicken exit. You can only support them when you know what they are."

John and Jake shared as openly as they were willing to after meeting only a few hours earlier. The time flew by, and they found themselves up against the clock, as the seminar was about to begin again. Not wanting to be late and face Dan's questioning, they returned to the room immediately.

Dan went to the front of the room and began talking about supporting one another. He asked everyone, "If you had walked up to a lake and out onto a dock and you saw a man drowning, what would you do? If there was a life ring attached to the rail and the life ring had a rope, what would you do?"

There were many different answers Jake could respond with, but it seemed to him there was only one thing to do. He was looking back at his own experience as a teenager when he had been trained to be a lifeguard at the local swimming pool. The answer seemed simple to Jake. You take the life ring, and you swim out with it, and you have the person who is drowning grab onto it, and you bring them back to shore.

Some people said you throw it out. It's got a rope on it. Let them grab the ring and pull them into shore. Others didn't know what to do other than to call for help.

"All these answers are good," Dan said. "Yet every one of them is derived from a judgment. Do I help you because you and I are the same color? Do I help you because you and I have the same religion? Do I help you because you and I make a lot of money, and we wouldn't associate with people who may not be at our financial level? I hope you have the same education. What was the real reason I would help you?"

Then, Dan said, "It boils down to this: we're all human and deserve our life on this planet. If someone is drowning, how can we help him or her?" He looked at the participants and said, "In some area of your life, every person in this room is drowning."

Jake wondered in what areas of his life was he drowning? He hadn't worked for two years, so he was drowning because he hadn't brought income in for the family. He'd been drowning because his wife was the sole income earner. He was drowning from lack of a close relationship with either of his two children. There were so many areas he could see where he was going under, and in some areas, it might be for the last time.

Dan then said, "I'm going to give you a chance to help another human being. They are drowning, and it's up to you to throw the life ring. And the way you throw the life ring is you give open and honest feedback."

He explained feedback doesn't necessarily mean it's true. It doesn't mean it's false. Feedback is your individual experience of the other person. He continued by telling them each person would stand in front of a small group and speak on a topic for a couple of minutes. Then, the small group would give him or her feedback, not on what they shared but on the experiences each member of the group created around the person. The topics were interesting to Jake. "What's your relationship with your mother? What's your relationship with your father? How do you like to control people? If you get too close to me this weekend, how will I push you away?"

Each person stood, received their topic, and shared. At the end of their time, the small group gave them feedback from two different perspectives. The first involved the things the group felt held this person back. Things like coming across as dishonest. The person would say, "My experience of you is dishonest. My experience of you is lacking self-esteem. My experience of you is feeling unworthy." After a minute or so, Dan would stop the feedback, and the group would begin to give feedback from the other perspective of those things that move the person forward in their life and relationships.

The group gave amazing feedback. "My experience of you is brave. My experience of you is risk-taker. My experience of you is knowledgeable. My experience of you is confident. My experience of you is wisdom." As Jake watched the person standing there, receiving their feedback, he could see it hit them hard as they were becoming emotional.

When the person received the feedback holding them back, it was as though they already knew all those things and accepted what was being said. It made no difference to them. But when they received the feedback that moved them forward, it struck an emotional chord in each person. Some people had their knees buckle. It was as though the feedback hit them so hard, and they almost crumbled to the floor. *How in the world could strangers, after only a few hours, know these things about you?* Things had to be true because they were experiencing them about you.

Dan wrapped up the day by asking if they had ever seen spider monkeys or knew what they were. Jake and Grace had spent time in Costa Rica, where they had seen spider monkeys in trees during a river cruise, so he knew what they were. Dan said the native people of some countries captured spider monkeys. They would sell them as pets, and they would also eat them as a delicacy.

But there was a method they used to capture the spider monkeys because they spend their time way up in the trees, and they were fast. The natives gathered coconuts, cut a hole in the top, dumped the liquid out, and put some rice down inside. Each coconut would be tied with a rope and a wooden stake. They took the coconuts out into the jungle clearing where they would stake the coconuts to the ground, all over the clearing. Then, the natives would go and hide. It wasn't long before the spider monkeys came out of the trees. The monkeys would take their little paw, and they'd push it down into the coconut and grab onto the rice. Holding the rice tightly in their paw, they tried to escape with the loot they had grabbed. Because they were holding the loot so tightly in their little fist, they couldn't get their paw out.

The natives would come out of hiding, gather the spider monkeys, and take them to the market. Dan asked the participants, "What is it from your past you're holding on to so tightly, you won't let go of it? What is keeping you from having all the desires of your heart?"

Jake felt like he was asking him directly.

The evening closed with homework assignments. Everyone was to engage in five minutes of prayer meditation and to journal on the emotional history of their life. They were to start from their earliest memory and write up to age fifteen. They were to journal at least three pages, more if they wanted.

It was not to be a chronological history but an emotional history. There were to be no dates and places where they lived. He wanted this journaling to be about the emotional side only. For clarity, he said journaling was much different than writing a letter.

Journaling a page involved writing from the top line to bottom line, margin to the edge of the page, no paragraphs, no spaces, no indentation. It was all-inclusive. Next, they were to write the names of ten people they felt had influenced their lives. He wanted them to look at a full range of ways people could influence. If they didn't remember the person's name, it was okay to write the situation down, only a sentence or two about it. Next, everyone was to write a commitment statement. The form of the statement was "I am committed to …" They were to fill it in with two to four qualities they were committed to bringing out in themselves during the week.

Jake and John said goodnight to each other, and Jake went to his room with Grace. He decided he would go ahead and do the homework before he'd go to bed, not realizing what was going to come up for him.

As he began to write, he noticed everything he was writing had to do with negative emotions. Why were they so prevalent in his life? Being brought up in the kind of family and atmosphere he had, negativity was all he had in his well of memories. Jake could not remember a single moment he had experienced happiness as a child, nor happiness in the family. There were times when they might pack a picnic and take off into the desert. The family wouldn't get very far before his father would pick a fight with his mother, and they would turn around and go back home, and the picnic wouldn't happen. So many of those kinds of events were flooding into his memory. It wasn't long before he realized he had gone well beyond three pages of journaling.

The next morning, Jake met with his buddy John. They had breakfast together, and they talked and compared their experiences of the day before. Jake suspected they were still trying to measure each other up, and they weren't open and honest with one another. Time seemed to fly, and it was time for the seminar to begin. Everyone gathered at the doors, having experienced what being late was the day before. The doors opened, and there was a rush of people to get in the room. Sure enough, some people didn't make it to their seats on time. Jake wondered what Dan would do today, because yesterday, he had climbed all over them for their tardiness.

Dan didn't miss a beat. He called them out by name and worked them through a process of finding out why they were late. They still had zero commitment to being on time. They were very lackadaisical experiences for these people, and Dan drilled down to learn what it was in their life that caused them to choose to be casual over being committed. From the other side of the room, Tom yelled, "Casualness breeds casualties. All you have to do is look around your life to see the casualties, the carnage you have left in your wake."

Once everyone was seated, the song, *Solitaire*, was played. For Jake, it was an emotional experience to sit there and listen to the song. People on either side of him were breaking down, and he was feeling his own emotions, knowing he had lived much of his life in the solitude of his mind. What was he going to do to shift his life so he could be in control of creating a life of his dreams?

Dan opened the floor for sharing. A woman shared about her time as a small child locked up in a storage room where coal was stored, fed only once a day. Another woman shared her dad had physically and sexually abused her since she was seven. These were stories that broke your heart.

Jake remembered from his childhood the neighbors would brutalize the one boy in the family. There were six girls in the family and one boy, but the boy could never do anything right. His mother would often bind his hands and feet and hang him in the cold smokehouse behind the home. He would scream and yell for help, and Jake recalled those sounds of him screaming and yelling, asking for help, but no one came. How could humanity do these things to one another? Even in his own family, his mother's brutalization by his father was something that should never have been allowed to continue for 28 years.

These were stories people had never told anyone. The shares were so gut-wrenching, and Jake was amazed at the similarities in the stories. He no longer felt alone for the first time in his life. Jake felt a kinship with these people who had walked a similar path through life as he had. He felt their pain of being lost and alone.

When the person had finished sharing, Dan asked them what they were committed to in the relationship with their buddy. What have they learned about them, and what would they help them create during the week?

Dan concluded his questioning with "are you 100% committed to your buddy winning this week? Without exception, each person declared they were committed to their buddy. Jake knew his buddy John was in a real struggle with his identity. He was struggling with being a gay man, and with so many areas of his life, Jake wasn't sure which one he could help him with the most. In the relationship, he wanted to learn more about a gay man to see if it could help him with his son.

Dan asked another buddy pair if they had spent any time together during the morning. Did they have breakfast together? Had one called the other to make sure they weren't going to be late? What kind of support had they given out in the hallway? Then, he said, "Did you check your buddy's homework?"

Jake thought, *Why would I need to check my buddy's homework?* Dan asked who wanted to play a bigger game, who wanted to take a big risk in the class? A couple of men jumped up and said they did. So, Dan invited them to the front of the room and explained the bigger game was playing as if your life depended on the answer from your buddy. Were they willing to put their life on the line and be dependent on their buddy's answer?

Both men said they were willing to play, so Dan asked one of the men, "Did your buddy complete his homework per our instructions?"

The first man thought for a moment and then said, "I believe he did. Yes, I think he did."

Dan asked, "Did you check it? Did you look at his homework in the hallway? Did you ask him if he completed it?"

The man responded, "No, I didn't, but I trust him."

"Oh," Dan said, "you have already developed some level of trust with your buddy, so you're willing to put your life on the line for him."

"Yes, I am willing," he said.

Dan turned to the other buddy, and he said, "Well, the same question goes to you, and this is as if your life depends on it. Did your buddy do his homework?"

The second buddy looked at the first one intently and said, "I don't know what I'm going to say. He did. He trusts me to have completed mine. I'm going to say he completed his."

Dan said, "Well, let's see. Let's take a look at the three pages of journaling."

They opened their notebooks up, and Dan barely took a glance at them and said, "You're dead. You're both dead. Your life depended on your answer, and your answer is inaccurate, and I can tell you right now, you're both dead. Your buddy did not complete his homework per our instructions." He yelled out to the rest of the participants, "What were the instructions for the three pages of journaling?"

It was as though the participants all heard different instructions. Jake had written them down and he knew they were to write three pages of journaling. Dan had said they could journal more, but three pages fulfilled the assignment. He clarified what a page of outside journaling looked like again. Jake was clear on it. Some people had written them down but had written different instructions than were given. *How did they hear those things?* he wondered.

Dan asked if they had ever been scuba diving. Some raised their hand, including Jake. Dan asked, "What's the first thing you do before you go underwater?"

Jake called out, "You get a buddy."

Dan responded, "Correct. And what do you do before you take your buddy underwater?"

"You check their equipment," someone else shouted out.

"Why do you check?"

"Because their life is on the line," another person shouted. "You're both going under the water, and if one of you has a problem, it's going to be the other one that helps to save your life."

"In this exercise, checking your buddy's homework is like checking your equipment before you go scuba diving,"

Dan said. "What you guys did here is you got to the 99th yard and stopped." He went on to explain what everyone had done was natural and what people usually do. They play it safe rather than take a risk in their relationships and dig in, choosing to play a surface level game. He called it a sandlot game, explaining there were two ways of playing the game for the rest of the week. They could play at the sandlot level, which they were already doing, or play at what he called an Olympic level.

He asked everyone, "Which level do you want to play at?"

Well, of course, everyone wanted to play at the Olympic level. He stopped the seminar and said it was up to the team to correct all the issues with the homework. Then, as a group, they were to create a team commitment statement.

The format of the commitment statement was "we, team 34, are committed to ..." Then, he instructed them to fill it in with two to four qualities the entire team was committed to bringing out during the rest of the week. Dan told them they didn't have long, and when they were complete, they were to let one of the staff members know. He stressed the need for urgency to correct the matter.

The team was in this predicament because they didn't keep their word when it came to the ground rules. They didn't keep their agreements with their buddy, with themselves, or with the team. They didn't follow instructions. He reminded the team they had said they were a 100% committed the day before. He said, "It's easy to talk, but it is much more difficult to put your words into action."

With those parting words, Dan, Tom, and Donna all left the room. Everybody sat there staring at each other. It wasn't long before someone stood up and called Jake by name. "Jake, would you lead us through this process?"

Jake looked around and said, "Why are you picking me to lead you?"

The young woman responded, "Because I trust you. You seem to be a man of integrity. And I'd like for you to be the one to lead us."

Jake stood up, looked around the room, and asked, "Is there anyone here who would object to what I've been asked to do? No one here really knows me. Some of you experienced me in our earlier class, but no one here, outside of Grace, knows me. So, if anyone objects and feels I'm not the one to take the lead of the room, please speak up."

Nobody objected. Jake went to the front of the room, and he began a conversation that lasted for more than five hours.

It seemed everyone had an opinion about how to get the homework done, but no one was willing to listen to one another. One person would stand up and give his or her opinion about how it should be done, and then the next person would stand up. It was as though they were dismissing each other's suggestions, and Jake was getting frustrated.

For five and a half hours, the process continued until finally, as a group, they had come together. They completed the homework accurately and created their commitment statement.

Dan, Tom, and Donna all returned to the room and began to work with them as though nothing had happened. The team had gotten back in agreement as far as Dan was concerned, so it was time to move on. It was as though there was no point in dwelling on the past.

What an interesting concept, Jake mused. *Dwelling on the past gets you nowhere, and now that it's been corrected, move on.*

The morning had been brutal. Everyone was tired, hungry, and needed to go to the bathroom. Dan called for everyone to go on a meal break, but it would be different than the previous one. He asked everyone to go with the small group created the night before when they gave feedback. They were to spend time together at lunch, learning more about one another. Jake and his group found a restaurant, and they went right to work on the task.

Soon, lunch was over, and the seminar restarted. They had been instructed to go to a different room in the hotel after they returned. It was a huge ballroom in another part of the hotel. Jake noticed the chairs had been set up in a specific way, and in front of the chairs, three scaffold platforms had been erected. They were the kind of platforms that might be used on a construction site. He wondered what was going to take place here tonight.

Dan took his place at the front of the room and began a lecture called a conversation for commitment. He said a request for commitment always begins with a question from the other party.

"What's in it for me?"

People seem to make commitments for a lot of reasons. Some of the most common ones are money, recognition, and cause. He pointed out cause was something you can't buy. It was not something you can manipulate people into. Cause was something people did because they believed in it, reminding everyone when people believe in something, they give their life or take the life of others. He used the example of how the Nazis killed six million Jews, saying they didn't do it for money or recognition. They did it because of the commitment they had to their cause.

Dan finished his lecture and asked everyone to gather around one of the platforms as he explained what they were going to do next. The exercise they were going to be taken on was a team exercise called trust fall. He explained each person would make a declaration to their team while on the floor.

The declaration would include the qualities they were committed to bringing out in themselves before they went up to the platform. Once on top of the platform, each person would move to the edge of the platform and turn their back to their team. When they were ready, they fell backward off the platform and were caught by their team members. They would be caught in the arms of their team members standing across from one another with their arms stretched out, creating a place for the person to land safely. Jake had never seen this done before, but he knew it was possible.

The exercise turned out to be a very emotional exercise for most people in the room, including Jake. He had never put his safety in the hands of anyone else. He couldn't trust people, so this was taking one of his biggest risks, but he declared at the earlier seminar he would begin to trust, and he was transforming himself into a trusting man. As he stood on a platform with his back to the team, he wanted in the worst way to look and make sure they were all set up and properly placed so his safety was assured.

The moment came when Jake leaned back and fell into the arms of his teammates, who easily caught him. He couldn't believe it. People who didn't know him a few hours earlier made sure he was safe. Emotions rose in Jake as he lay in their arms and felt their support. He released the emotion lying there, and they held him as though he was the most important person in their lives. Jake noticed the team was coming closer and closer together. They physically would stand closer together. Their energy was expanding surrounding one another. It was as though they had found a brother, sister, or a family member who had been long lost, and Jake felt a part of it.

The day's session was closed with everyone in his or her small group, and a final song called "When You Put Your Heart in It" by Kenny Rogers was played. The song seemed perfect for this moment. The team had come together, and they had worked together during the trust fall exercise where they trusted one another. Everyone, including Jake, had trusted themselves and put their safety in the hands of someone else.

Day number three began with a song by Mike and the Mechanics called "The Living Years." Jake had heard it many times and connected with the song, but in this space and context, it hit him hard when it was played. He doubled over with emotion. People on either side of him reached out to try and comfort him. But Jake was overcome with emotion because he realized he'd never really reconciled with his dad. Still, the greater pain he experienced was the lack of reconciliation between him and his two children.

What would his final hours be like in his life? What would people say about him? Would he ever be able to reconcile the differences between him and his son and daughter? The song played, and Jake wept through the entire song. Grace would later say she had noticed Jake from across the room, and her heart was broken because he was in such pain, and she knew what the song meant to him. It pained her to watch him suffer so.

The room was filled with a lot of emotion from the team. At the end of the song, Dan asked everyone to go back to the small groups they had been in the last couple of days. He explained they were going to do a new exercise. It was an exercise where the participants had to be honest with them. The room was darkened, and Dan was going to ask questions. If the question or statement was true for them in any way, all they needed to do was raise their hand. With the room darkened and everyone's eyes closed, they had privacy, so no one would see them raise their hands.

He asked some very intimate questions. "Have you ever been raped? Have you abused alcohol or drugs as a child? Were you abused as a child? Have you ever cheated or stolen from someone or your company? Have your ever taken credit for someone else's achievement? Have you ever hit or abused a spouse or relationship?"

At the end of the question and response exercise, everyone was instructed to share something from their past. They could share something from the questions and statements Dan had asked, or they could share something completely different. It was the time to share a secret they may have never shared with another person.

The exercise was cathartic for everyone. Jake felt like he had played full out in the exercise, and he had gained much by being honest and transparent. He had been experiencing feelings and emotions he had never felt before, but all of that was to prepare him for what was coming next.

After returning from a break, Jake noticed the room had been reset, and it looked completely different. Chairs were in small groups, and they'd be seated in their chairs, facing away from each other in the circle.

Jake was ready to take on whatever they were going to throw at him.

The next exercise turned out to be one where each person in the room would have a simulated experience of their death after suddenly being struck with an illness and ending up in the hospital. Each person would learn his or her death was imminent. They would only have enough time to talk to some dear friends and a few family members. Each person would be in the experience of dying. A friend would come in and share with them and cry with them. A brother or a sister would come in, and their mother and father would finally go in and wipe the tears from their face. The cathartic release in the room was overwhelming, with some people getting sick and throwing up and others falling to the floor as they wept.

The exercise was incredibly powerful for Jake. He had never thought about his mortality, yet here he was facing it as though it was real. The moment came when everyone in the exercise would take their last breath, after which they metaphorically passed on to the other side. The exercise was completed with everyone writing about their experience and if they had felt like they had been given a message when they passed to the other side. The message, Dan explained, was tied to their purpose in life. *What am I going to do with my message?* Jake wondered.

<hr />

The final experiences of the evening centered around a martial art known as Aikido. Though he had heard of many martial arts, Aikido was new to him. A Japanese martial arts practitioner, Morihei Ueshiba, had become a master in so many different martial arts that he decided to create his own, naming it Aikido. Dan said they would be in the practice of being grounded and centered, and he would go through the different variations of how one would ground and center themselves, and then they would be in the experience of maintaining ground and center in different exercises.

The first exercise he called the push. The push was a representation of someone coming at you, physically ranting and raving. Jake had experienced that many times in his business career, especially with the union business agent. He'd come into his office and rant and rave about some action the company had taken, which he felt was not fair for his members. If someone was being fired, the business agent sometimes tried to make it sound like they were fired unjustly, screaming, yelling, and cursing.

Jake had seen and experienced these kinds of situations many times, but in this exercise, when one remained grounded and centered, all the noise, all the chaos seemed to pass by. It didn't have any effect on Jake. In the past, Jake would have met the rants and raves with a matching voice, tone, and energy. But staying grounded and centered, he didn't feel he was being attacked. It was incredible for him to experience such a thing after all those decades of pushing back and fighting.

Dan explained when people are pushed, they push back, and it's a pushback that came from something in their childhood. Some experience in their childhood when he or she was abused mentally, physically, or emotionally, and he or she tried to survive by pushing back. By being grounded, centered, and allowing all the chaos to go around him or her, there was no need to push back.

The next exercise was called the shout. The shout looked like two people standing face to face, close enough they were really in each other's space without touching, and they would take a deep breath, and one at a time, they shouted into the face of the other person. The other person's job was to remain grounded and centered and not let the noise and the chaos of the shout cause them to deviate from being grounded and centered.

The participants took turns shouting at each other. The experience was as though the noise coming at them separated itself and went around them. By remaining grounded, one could hardly even hear the shout. Those who lost being grounded and centered moved either backward or leaned into the shout. Dan explained these were representations of giving up or pushing back.

Next came the pass, where two people walked toward one another. Then, as they approached face to face, almost in a two-step dance, they would turn and walk backward from each other in opposite directions. It was quite beautiful to watch these new people step into an exercise they've never done before and, within minutes, seemingly master it. Dan threw in a couple of little extra things, one of which he called hard eyes and soft eyes.

Jake stared intently into his partner's eyes, almost like having tunnel vision. He could see what was directly in front of him, but he couldn't see anything else. Then, Dan asked them to soften their brow and allow their vision to expand. As Jake allowed his brow to relax, his view of the room opened, and he could see everything. Even though he was looking directly at the person, he could see the floor, the walls, the ceiling, and the people around him.

The team didn't realize Dan was setting them up for the final exercise of the evening. The exercise was a simulation game in fourteenth-century Japan, a time when there were lords of the land called daimyo.

Jake was certain after the previous day's efforts of trying to lead his team through a five-hour shut down, it was not likely he'd be selected to be the leader of his group. As expected, Jake was not selected to be the daimyo. One of the other participants was selected, but the daimyo selected Jake to be his sentry. Jake was placed in front of the entire army on his side of the battlefield to keep a lookout for anything that could affect his army so he could report it back to his daimyo.

It seemed like a very honorable position to be placed in, and Jake would do it with his full heart.

The simulation was filled with moral dilemmas everyone faces in their life, and it had many, many layers. There was no clear answer as to why people did what they did in the simulation. It was like the Game of Life Jake played during the previous seminar he had attended. You go into the world, you bring peace and joy, you share compassion, and you show others how to step into forward-moving compassionate action by taking risks.

Day four began early in the morning, with the team meeting at 6:30 a.m. to gather and get on buses to be taken to another location where they would be outdoors all day. The location happened to be in a redwood forest where a company had created a high-ropes course the team would be challenged on all day. They would face their fears, their commitments to take risks, and find resourcefulness within themselves.

Part of the day was a buddy exercise, and part of the day was a team exercise, but it would begin with an individual exercise. The guides for the high-ropes challenge course explained how they would use harnesses and ropes to protect people, but it was up to each person to do the exercise. The exercise wasn't so much about the physical elements in front of the person, but it was about what the person would bring out of him or herself to overcome anything that could hold them back from completing the exercise. Jake was assigned the first exercise with a small group of people who would climb a 40-foot pole, a redwood tree that had been topped, and had a small round disk mounted on the top.

Some would climb and stand on the top, while others might only climb part way or not at all. Regardless, they were responsible for creating their own experiences throughout the day. Those who climbed and stood on the disk would stand there for a few seconds, turn around, and jump off into nothingness toward a trapeze bar hanging in front of them. The trapeze bar represented their future, a goal or vision the person had set. Reaching the trapeze and grabbing onto it was a metaphor for having achieved their goal.

Jake had climbed many ladders in his career. He'd been at many high places, so climbing the pole, physically, was not a challenge for him, but getting on top and standing there on such a small area, nine inches in diameter or so, Jake felt fear rise inside of himself. He had ropes on his harness, so even if he fell off, he knew he'd be caught. But the fear was overcoming the knowledge he was safe. It took some time while on top of the pole to turn around and face the trapeze. Giving it all his effort, he leaped into the air but missed catching the trapeze. His hand touched it, but he couldn't grab it.

For Jake, it was very disheartening because it was as though he had failed to achieve his dream, but in fact, he hadn't failed. He had achieved more than he could have had he not climbed the pole or had not jumped off. He witnessed others who climbed the pole, jumped, and grabbed the trapeze and others who missed the trapeze. The day was filled with ideas of what people claimed success and failure looked like.

The next exercise was a buddy exercise. Jake and John climbed two adjacent trees simultaneously. When they got up about 40 feet off the ground, two cables were strung between the two trees on one side of the area and two other trees on a far side of the area. The cables were strung into a V-pattern between the trees. The instruction was to stand on the cables and to reach out to one another at the top of the ladder and to put their hands on each other's shoulders and then to move out across the cables as far as they could go.

When they started, Jake noticed they were standing straight up, and their hands were on each other's shoulders. As they moved farther and farther out across the cables, their bodies began to layout flatter and flatter because the cables were spreading, and their feet were getting farther apart from one another. The farther out they moved and the flatter they became, the less support they felt from each other. Jake compared this to his relationship with his family. They were getting further and further apart and not experiencing support from one another.

It wasn't long before John and Jake lost their connection and fell off the cables. The safety ropes caught them, so they didn't fall far, and they were let down slowly to the ground. On the way down, Jake reached out and grabbed hold of John and brought him in close and hugged him tightly. John hugged back, and as they stood on the ground, the entire team surrounded them and cheered for them, saying they had moved farther out on the cable than either Jake or John thought. It wasn't about how far you went; it was about the support given to each other to get to the place. Jake was beginning to realize, like his relationship with Martin, he had not been giving him support, and they were both still basically stuck on the ground. They hadn't taken the first step and climbed the ladder.

The final exercise of the day was facing a vertical wall that was about fourteen feet tall. The objective was to get everyone from the ground up and over the wall. Jake instantly could see solutions in his mind of how to do it. But there were people in the group who had already experienced something similar, from cheerleaders to military people. There were specific instructions that would protect everyone, keeping them safe.

So, the way the military guys experienced a similar wall wouldn't work. The way the cheerleaders had experienced a similar exercise was unsafe, so they couldn't use the process. Jake and his group had to come together as a team and figure out how they would accomplish the goal with the instructions given and in the limited time they had. They had to leave before sunset to get out of the redwoods safely.

In a short time, the team came up with the strategy of how to get everybody up and over the wall. They had already picked the first person going up to help the next person over. When it came to Jake's turn to go up and over the wall, he resisted because he felt he was stronger than most people on the ground, and he could better serve them by being on the ground and pushing people up. But it was his turn, and the group had decided he was going next, so he was raised off the ground. Jake reached up for support, and in an instant, he realized this was not what his business career looked like. He hadn't felt the support of the people he worked with or for and not from those that had gone before him or those who were his employees.

Yet here it was, people on the ground were supporting him to achieve a goal that had been taken on, and people up above were reaching down for him to help bring him over the wall. In a flash, Jake realized his leadership had been less effective than it could have been had he not been so fear-driven and manipulating people to get what he wanted. By being more service-minded, helping others achieve their goals, they would help him achieve his.

Throughout the entire day, the experience at the wall would be one that Jake would remember for the rest of his life. Though he could not go back and change how he had been, he could become a different person going forward. One that was more service-minded, servant leadership oriented versus one that was about doing it all his way. The day would end with a great celebration with the entire team back at the hotel.

The Grand Ballroom had been transformed into a great dining hall, and everyone was excited to go, dressed in the best clothing they had brought. The team entered the Grand Ballroom, where a celebration was waiting for them.

Photographers had taken candid photos of the team members since the trust fall evening and had put together slides showing team members in their candid moments of greatness. Everybody loved, cheered, and cried at their moments of achievement and the experiences that filled their hearts to overflowing with joy, happiness, and love. The team had bonded. They'd come together. It was as though they were operating as one, and Jake felt he had found lifelong family and friends.

Day five, the last day of the seminar, started with an exercise Dan called design your life. Jake thought that was not something he had ever taken on but was willing to do. They were to write about their career, money, relationship, spiritual walk, and their health. They could write anything they wanted, but the idea was to design their life in those areas as though they had already created them. They were to make them a risk, to make them beyond what they thought they could do and something they were committed to taking on. He would only give him a few minutes to do this, so there was much urgency to be brought to the exercise.

Next, he had everyone take out money and hold it in her hands, asking them, "What does money mean? What is money anyway?"

Someone said, "Money is an agreement."

Another said, "It is paper, which could be used for many different things."

Dan asked everyone to look at the money, to stare at the face on the money. He said, "If you stare hard enough and long enough, you would probably see the lips moving." After a moment, he asked everyone to listen to the money. "What is it saying to you?"

Some of the answers Jake heard surprised him. People were saying such things as you don't deserve me; you don't have enough of me; you can't keep me. All Jake could think of was *I must work hard for my money.* It was the only thing he had ever known and the only thing he had ever worked for.

Dan asked, "From whom do we learn the most about money?" It was from our parents, the people who raised us. How were they with money? What did they believe about money? Those were the same things Jake picked up from his parents, and they were likely the same things holding him back.

And then, Dan asked a strange question, "What are rich people?"

The answers the team threw out were astounding. Rich people are stingy. Rich people are arrogant. Rich people are mean and on and on. Without taking a pause, Dan yelled out, "Who wants to be rich?"

Everybody raised his or her hand. Jake looked around the room with his hand in the air, realizing his judgment of rich people was counter to his desire to be rich. Dan pointed out if you truly felt this way about people who had great wealth, how could you ever become one of those people you already judged and didn't like? Dan told them if they didn't have a burning desire for their dreams, they could never achieve their goals. They could think about them, want them, wish for them, desire them, but without a burning desire, something that moves them to act toward their dreams and goals, they would never see them manifested in their lives.

He reminded everyone of day number one when he talked about people being more committed to hanging on to their past than they were to achieve their dreams and goals. Reminding them that some people hang onto first base, hoping to create what they want but never taking a risk and leaving their first base. They were more committed to something other than their dreams and goals.

Jake knew that change was going to be difficult. He'd been trying to change for decades and had never been successful. In this exercise, he hoped he would gain the tools and the techniques for creating a deep and lasting change: a transformation he could use to rocket his life forward to achieve greater results and have an incredible life with his wife and children.

LOOKING BACK:

Before the exercise was over, Jake came to realize he had put on many poses and many acts so people would believe he had things all figured out. Those poses did tend to work for him when he was a kid, but as an adult, they no longer created his desired results. Jake realized he was more committed to appearing honest to others so that he would gain their respect, trust, and acceptance than to go after his dreams and goals.

How do you transform your life when you have something so deeply anchored in your unconscious mind that you never know when it's going to fire off?

Jake soon realized he would have to make choices moment by moment to overcome his unconscious programming that was stronger than his desires for the life he wanted.

Jake and Grace returned home with a renewed energy and a passion for each other, their marriage, and for life in general.

YOUR INTROSPECTIVE CHALLENGE:

1. What awareness came up for you as you read this chapter?

    _____

    _____

    _____

    _____

2. What would you change if you could go back in time?

    _____

    _____

    _____

    _____

3. What action can you take today to shift?

    _____

    _____

    _____

    _____

4. What, if anything, will result if you do not shift?

    _____

    _____

    _____

    _____

VIII

OUR HEART'S DESIRES

In this world, there are only two tragedies.
One is not getting what one wants, and
the other is getting it.

—Oscar Wilde, "Lady Windermere's Fan:
A Play about a Good Woman"

L ooking back over Jake's life, it is easy to say he had been dealt a lousy hand he had to play out and born into a family who had only known poverty and victimhood. He watched and listened to his parents and older siblings interact with groups of people and learned some were treated with respect, while others were disliked, even hated, and disparaged. He learned and came to believe, the only way to create money was to work extremely hard and sacrifice his dreams. His understanding of what being in a relationship meant was more like being entangled with another person than connection. Jake learned to trust someone was to set in motion many opportunities for being hurt, physically, emotionally, and mentally. After experiencing that kind of pain, when his parents divorced, he hardened himself so no one could hurt him so deeply again.

The truth of how Jake's life unfolded resulted from unintentional, unconscious programming. Not of his doing but, rather, the programming passed down from generation to generation by his parents and others who had authority over him as a child. How does this happen such that an individual is completely unaware, you might be wondering? Have you ever been doing something, then suddenly, you become aware, consciously, of a negative thought about somebody or circumstance? Likely, you have and wondered why that kind of thought would pop into your mind at that moment. As I addressed at the beginning of this book, 95% of our subconscious programming is in place by the age of seven, including much of the negative programming you will unconsciously draw upon throughout your life. A child isn't self-aware enough to process all that occurs around him or her until about age eight. It's as though they are in a hypnotic state and absorbing, in their unconscious mind, everything said and done by those in their environment.

In the Theta state of mind, which occurs right before deep REM sleep and before awakening, the mind can learn profound and complex content.[5] If you have ever worn a headset or had a meditative recording playing as you slept, you were inputting, into your unconscious mind, the content of the recording. This is what happens to children from birth to age seven. The man or woman you are today is a direct result of your childhood programming. It can be unnerving to learn much of our negative, instant responses to life's circumstances are generated in our unconscious programming. As an adult, you can find comfort in knowing it isn't you. It is the unconscious mind of the small child who still lives inside your mind and is programmed with so many negative programs. These programs, connected to powerful emotions you experienced throughout your childhood, make most of your unintended, gut-level responses in life.

Consider for a moment that 95% of your daily thoughts are subconsciously playing out in every decision and action you take. That only leaves you five percent consciousness for being creative and intentional about the life you want to live. If you are like me, the hundreds of interruptions in my day reduce that small amount of consciousness, including the times when my mind begins to wander, replaying negative thoughts I have and have had before.

One of Jake's greatest desires was to have loving, respectful, honest, and open relationships with his children. His subconscious programming didn't have the blueprint or schematic for creating those relationships. He was not raised in that kind of family, so he had nothing to draw from that could support him in creating the kinds of relationships he longed for. Jake had to come to grips with his judgments of others and his wounds related to abandonment and betrayal. He had to be willing to be coached and called out any time one of his programs was projecting messaging contrary to what he believed he was projecting. His journey to becoming authentic was painful and gut-wrenching. The result was what he wanted, but he had no idea what it would look like. It was heartbreaking and painful to watch his children make their journey harder and filled with painful prices. Like most parents, Grace and Jake wanted more for their children so they could have a far better life than they had.

As challenging as it was to be in a relationship with his son, Jake's daughter, Renee, had built an impervious barrier around her. She married a man whose known infidelity had resulted in a child with another woman. During a time before they married, Jake had told her fiancée he would never control Renee. "She is a woman with her way of doing things and is not easily persuaded otherwise," he said.

Their 15-year marriage was tormenting for Grace and Jake to witness. They had three children and did what they could to parent them, but coming from quite different family dynamics and cultures, it was an uphill journey. Drew, her husband, grew up in a family with an 80-year history of only male babies being born. His mother and father adopted a girl after five boys were born to them. Renee birthed a girl in her third pregnancy, which was something to celebrate for both sides of their family.

The turmoil between Renee and Drew increased with each passing day, resulting in more infidelity. Renee regularly went to a bar with open gambling and lost large sums of her income. She continued drinking and gambling, numbing the pain she was experiencing.

For almost 20 years, Renee hid out from being in a relationship with Grace and Jake. Even when they were together, Jake kept his distance because he knew she was not open to being honest with him. In the year Grace and Jake had attended their first seminar, Renee and Drew reluctantly agreed to attend. Jake was disappointed in them both, as they didn't engage and avoided taking part in most of the exercises. Together, they would hide in a corner or up against a wall to become invisible. However, in the end, when the opportunity was offered to take the next level of training, Renee agreed to go. Jake and Grace were excited for her and wanted Renee to experience the life-transforming breakthroughs they had experienced.

She attended the next level within weeks of registering. Grace and Jake signed up to be volunteer staff after talking to Tom, the seminar company owner, about supporting her. Tom had become a valued friend and mentor to Jake, and he always answered Jake's questions honestly. He responded to them, saying, "Why wouldn't you want to be there?" Neither of them could give a good reason besides feeling their presence might hinder her from being fully engaged. Tom assured them. Regardless of how she chose to engage, she would get what she needed from the weeklong seminar.

Because so much of the work done in this intensive seminar is completed in small groups, it wasn't obvious Renee was engaged and gaining the benefits of her time there. However, on the evening of day three, Renee was chosen to be in a battle called the Graceful Dancer during the battle stimulation. When she walked onto the floor, Grace and Jake knew she was terrified to be seen so publicly, exposed to others' judgments and comments behind her back. Somewhere deep within her being, Renee brought forth the courage and fortitude needed to perform the battle with grace, beauty, and skill. Jake and Grace sobbed tears of joy as they watched her surrender and bring forth her authentic being for possibly the first time in her adult life.

The next day, it was outdoors in the Redwood Forest, where Renee's newly revealed state of being would manifest a whole and healed woman. She engaged fully in all the exercises, offered and gave her teammates support when they needed her the most. Renee had broken free from her self-imposed prison and was experiencing passion like she never had. Much like Jake after his first seminar, she demonstrated what it was like to have a heart on fire for life and others.

At the end of the day, when the team was sharing about their experience, Renee stood and addressed her team.

Through tears, she related she had always judged herself harshly because of her size, thinking of herself as "a heifer." The facilitators and the guides had provided the team with many opportunities for breakthroughs, and it seemed Renee had created hers. Addressing Jake and Grace, she said, "Mom, Dad, I'm sorry if you disapprove, but this is the real me. Good-bye, heifer, hello, butterfly!" Their hearts leaped with joy for Renee. Finally, she was being raw and real, which opened a doorway for creating a relationship her parents had dreamt of having with her.

For a while, Jake and Grace's relationship with Renee grew in positive ways. Returning home to the same culture and context she and Drew had created did not support her new passion for her life. It wasn't long, and she was back in the bars and gambling her paycheck away while drinking heavily to numb the pain of her relationship. Her marriage ended in an ugly and bitter divorce with Renee getting custody of her children. But her drinking and gambling and lack of good parenting were enough for Drew to sue for custody, which he won.

Renee was off the rails and headed in the direction of becoming homeless and without a job when she and Drew resolved their differences and got back together. After a few years of the same old struggles, they again separated, and Drew married another woman. They shared time with their children, but Renee wasn't dealing with her addictions and could not meet her financial obligations.

At the time of writing *Despite Me,* Renee has been married to Tony for eleven years. Tony loved Renee's children and didn't hesitate to give them the love and attention they needed. He had grown up without a father, though his mother had married three different times. He had deep wounds of abandonment and wanted the children to experience a loving and caring man they could depend upon. His addiction to drugs resurfaced, and soon, he and Renee were having similar issues as with her first marriage. Her gambling became routine, as did his drug use. Together, they were spiraling out of control. Bills were being ignored, rent wasn't paid on time, if at all, and they fought all the time. Their life together was tormenting for both, but neither was willing to seek the help they needed.

Out of the blue, Renee called Jake and Grace and said she wanted to meet them in her home. She seemed to have a lot to say but didn't want to do it over the phone. Reluctantly, they agreed, not sure what she might have to say or why it was so urgent. Without any hesitation, once they arrived, Renee began the conversation saying Tony had something he wanted to tell them. He had gotten into legal trouble and was facing a court date and wanted to come clean with Jake and Grace. He sobbed as he shared what he had done. Because Renee often gambled away her income, Tony felt his back was against the wall. His lawn care business didn't produce sufficient income to replace Renee's gambling losses, so he began to steal small amounts of metal to sell as scrap. With bills piling up, stealing became an easy way to create more money. He stole something of value from one of his clients, who reported the theft and filed a lawsuit for financial reparations. Jake wasn't surprised and said so. It seemed Tony had committed a similar crime against Jake and Grace years earlier. Not wanting to cause any deeper rift between them, Jake decided to let it go and not file a police report, thinking it would only cause greater problems between Renee and Tony.

It wasn't long into the conversation when Jake noticed something seemed off with Renee. She was making accusations and statements that weren't true. She had conferenced her brother into the conversation by phone, and he was also noticing she wasn't expressing herself with clarity. She kept saying she had a message from God to give, but it was all scrambled in her brain, and she couldn't express it clearly. When asked if she was on drugs or had started taking a new prescription, her response was an emphatic denial. But there were clear signs something was happening to her, even though she insisted she was fine. Grace and Jake spent much of the day with her and Tony. The conversation didn't resolve anything, so they decided to return home.

The following morning, Tony called, sounding like he was panicking. It seemed Renee was doing things that were very abnormal for her, and he was scared. Jake could hear Renee screaming in the background. He told Tony to call an ambulance and get her to the hospital immediately. He didn't know what was wrong, but he could hear enough to know Renee was out of control and might injure herself.

By the time she got to the hospital, she was calm and refused inpatient help, so they released her. Again, Tony called Jake and expressed his concern that she didn't get the help she needed and feared she would continue to have a problem. Jake stressed he needed to watch her closely throughout the day. He was sure Renee would revert to the out-of-control behavior that evening or the next day.

It wasn't very late in the day when Tony called Jake about Renee. She was much worse than in the morning, and Tony was afraid for her. She had kicked Tony several times and kicked their dog. He knew she loved him and would feel awful to realize she may have injured him. Jake instructed Tony to call the ambulance and call him back once they arrived.

A state trooper was in the area and answered the call first. Renee was overly aggressive and continued to demonstrate out-of-control behavior. She ripped the side mirror off her

SUV and picked up a piece of metal, one-handed, and threw it across the driveway and over her SUV. Tony said when he loaded the metal onto his trailer, he had to use both hands to lift it. As Tony and Jake were discussing next steps, two more sheriffs arrived. They also witnessed Renee's behavior and concluded drugs were the reason. They knew her personally and professionally and had never seen her in such a state. As they attempted to calm her, she attacked the state trooper's vehicle, which was enough to place her under arrest.

During the evening, Renee demonstrated outrageous acts she would never knowingly do. She was being monitored in an isolated cell, and those attending to her knew something wrong was happening with her. It wasn't long before a qualified evaluator was called in, and a short time later, Renee was admitted to the hospital under a 48-hour hold for further evaluation. The hospital didn't have the staff or facilities to care for a person in Renee's condition, so they searched the state until they found a place that would accept Renee. She was taken to a care facility some four hours from her hometown and admitted for care in a psychiatric facility. She was given medication to calm her down. After four days of inpatient treatment, she was released and returned home with Grace and Jake driving the eight-hour round trip. The long drive home allowed them all to engage as a family and learn more about what Renee had been experiencing.

LOOKING BACK:

In her work, Renee had experienced more trauma and drama than most people do in a lifetime. She was diagnosed with PTSD, which was triggered by an event causing her to believe she had put her and her family in life-threatening jeopardy. Jake remembered, during the first day they had met with her and Tony, Renee seemed terrified about an event tied to her work. She shared she was afraid she had put them in danger, and they could be killed if found out. The doctors diagnosed she had undergone an emotional meltdown due to post-traumatic stress and would need time to heal.

Whatever their daughter had experienced, it resulted in her state of being transforming moment by moment. She was engaging, open, raw, and real with them. She was doing the kinds of things a mother and wife would do in the home to care for her family. She was no longer gambling or drinking, but, rather, taking on hobbies, going to church, and celebrating her recovery. Renee had taken herself on with counseling for gambling, meeting with her doctor and her psychologist regularly. More and more often, she expressed her love and gratitude for her parents each time they were together.

Finally, Jake and Grace could be in a loving and accepting relationship with their daughter for the first time in decades. His dream of an open, honest, and intimate father and daughter relationship was being realized. The pain of their past had faded and seemed like a distant memory.

YOUR INTROSPECTIVE CHALLENGE:

1. What desire of yours has yet to be manifested?

    _____

    _____

    _____

    _____

2. What are the obstacles you must overcome?

    _____

    _____

    _____

    _____

3. What action steps can you take today that will move you toward your goal?

    _____

    _____

    _____

    _____

4. How have family and others impacted your progress?

    _____

    _____

    _____

    _____

PART III
BREAKTHROUGH

IX

REFRAMING OUR NARRATIVES

*Borges said there are only four stories to tell: a love story
between two people, a love story between three people,
the struggle for power and the voyage. All of us writers
rewrite these same stories ad infinitum.*

—Paolo Coelho

W hen you put a hundred people in a room and ask them
about their significant emotional events, you likely will
hear such things as divorce, abandonment, death, abuse,
and such matters of the heart. You can take any one of these
experiences and ask, "What did you make it mean about you?"

The answers are never the same. You can ask why. Is it
because nobody's life experience has an inherent meaning?
Everyone interprets events by filtering them through their
significant emotional experiences from childhood through
adulthood. We must make sense of these events, or they will

drive us insane. Once we have the interpretation, we will create a narrative that supports our interpretation of an event. And we'll go through life sharing our narrative with anyone who will listen. As we become so committed to our narrative, we seek new evidence to prove ourselves right.

During the three years Jake, Grace, Lucy, and Don had hosted dozens of evening workshops and three day seminars, Jake also attended a dozen of the five-day advanced-level seminars. He was gaining so much value he wanted more and wanted to support others in gaining the same for their lives. His role in the seminars was as a volunteer staff member: a role Jake came to love and see as some of the best training a graduate could get for the cost of travel expenses.

Soon, Jake was spending a great deal of time with the company's owner, vice presidents, salespeople, and facilitators. He became well known to them as a loyal and committed graduate of the company's programs. They spent time together in seminars and conferences outside of the owner's company, where they socialized and collaborated on business ideas and strategies.

While attending one such conference, Jake and Grace were approached by Donna, one of Tom's facilitators, and asked if they would be in prayer with her. Donna wanted to introduce a new seminar into the company, specifically for the Christian church community. She had already approached Lucy and Don, who had agreed to support her. Jake and Grace felt honored to be asked and included in Donna's inner circle of trusted friends.

Donna was searching for a name for this new seminar and had been stuck for some time. She had the material content and would be the only facilitator, so this was her remaining obstacle. After a dinner meeting, the five of them were together exchanging ideas, when Jake expressed his concern about coming up with a name quickly. Without any experience in this area, Jake said if she was looking for a quick answer, she might be disappointed as companies pay hundreds, if not thousands of dollars, at times, to develop branding and marketing for products, but he agreed he would pray for an answer. The evening ended with the five members of Donna's team entering into prayer about her request. They were in full agreement that coming up with a name for the new seminar was a priority.

The bed in the hotel was like lying down on a cloud. Whether they were exhausted from the day's events or the comfort of the bed, Jake was soon fast asleep. At 2:30 a.m., Jake was suddenly awakened by the clear sound of a voice. Believing someone was in his room, he sat straight up in bed, ready to pounce if needed.

"Jake, it's the quickening It's the quickening, Jake."

Sitting up, he looked around but didn't see anyone. Grace was still sound asleep, and besides, it was a male-sounding voice, so it wasn't her. Thinking it must have been someone walking down the hallway talking, Jake fell back asleep.

He hadn't been asleep for long when, again, he was awakened by the same voice saying, "Jake, it's the quickening. It's the quickening, Jake." This time, he launched out of bed and searched the room for where or from whom the voice was coming. But there wasn't anyone there except Grace and himself, and she was still sound asleep.

Thinking about those words, *the quickening*, he sat at the desk wondering what it meant. By now, he was wide-awake and knew sleep would not come easy for him after being awakened twice. He remembered reading the word, *quicken*, in Bible scriptures, so he began to look them up. In so many of the verses, the writer was in prayer, asking the Lord to quicken him or them. Why had this word come to Jake now, and how could he interpret it for any reason in his life?

Jake decided one way he might find an answer was to journal his experiences since he had met Tom and his team. He had attended all the organization's seminars, hosted many, and volunteered at dozens of others. Surely, his writing would reveal something meaningful so he could get back to sleep.

After writing for a couple of hours and a couple of dozen pages, he had a moment of clarity. What if this word, *quickening*, had something to do with the prayers Donna's team had prayed at the end of their meeting? Is it something she could use in her search for the branding? What if the branding was what Jake had heard, not once but four times in the night? He decided the best course of action was to share his notes with Donna and let her be the judge.

The morning came quickly, with only a few minutes for breakfast before the conference began. There wasn't enough time for Jake to have a formal meeting with the team, so when Donna walked into the conference room, he rushed to her. He was excited to share what had taken place during the night and wanted to give her his notes.

With a quick greeting, he couldn't contain his excitement and blurted out to Donna, "I have something for you."

She smiled broadly and asked him what it was.

"Notes from being awakened in the night after our meeting."

"Notes on what?" she asked.

Not being certain what he should say about them, he said, "I think it might be the name for your seminar."

Announcements were beginning, so there wasn't any more time to talk, so Jake asked Donna to take the notes and review them when she had time. They had a planned conference call with the prayer team in two weeks, and they could discuss the notes then.

Donna was a primary facilitator in Tom's organization, so she was on the road every week. When the prayer team came together on their call, Jake asked about her thoughts related to his notes and the name he had heard in his sleep and shared with her. Embarrassed, Donna disclosed she had not had time to read through the more than twenty pages of notes, but she would the following day.

Jake was sorely disappointed, believing he was the messenger with an important message to be delivered. This was one more disappointment in his lifetime of disappointments when it came to other people.

Three days passed and still no word from Donna. Had she even read his notes? She seemed to express that her need for a seminar brand was urgent, but she wasn't responding as though it was. The thoughts had barely crossed his mind when his phone rang.

It was Donna, and she was excited. "Jake, you're not going to believe this, but Tom and Dan have signed off on the name. I'm sorry it took so long for me to get back to you, but we've been in meetings, and they have agreed The Quickening is the perfect name for my new seminar."

Not in Jake's wildest dreams had he imagined the name he heard in his sleep would end up becoming the exact name of the seminar. Oh sure, some variation of it or a completely new and different name would come of it, but the exact name seemed like a crazy coincidence. Donna assured Jake she was not joking or kidding around, and they were already putting content on the website for her new seminar, known as The Quickening.

———∞∞∞———

During one of the dozens of Jake's staffing experiences, the facilitator, Bradley, approached Jake and said, "You know, Jake, you could be doing this." Jake must have looked confused because the facilitator repeated himself. "You could be doing this."

"Doing what?" Jake asked.

"What I'm doing, making a bigger difference for people." Without saying more, Bradley turned and walked back to the front of the room. Those few words struck a chord within him. He couldn't explain why, but he knew Bradley was right. During the next few hours of the training, all Jake could think about were those words: "You could be doing this." Then, Bradley wrote some words on a flip chart pad; Maximum Gain; participate; be open; be honest; trust; and take a big risk.

Bradley explained that to get maximum gain during the weekend, they would need to participate. Participation meant to engage, share, and contribute to the seminar—to be open to receiving and giving. To be honest with ourselves and everyone in the seminar and take a big risk with our emotions, feelings, and to be vulnerable.

As Jake listened and read through the list over and over, he realized he was not creating maximum gain in his life. Yes, he was a different man, but was he capitalizing on his transformation? He wondered. Like a blast of frigid winter air hitting him, he knew he wasn't creating maximum gain in his life, and there was no way he was creating it for others.

At the next break, Jake knew he had to speak out what he was thinking, so he approached Bradley and asked for a moment of his time. He looked him in the eyes and said, "You're right! I could be doing this, I should be doing this, and I commit to calling Tom—the owner—on Monday." It was a moment of clarity that would change Jake's future in ways he had not considered.

Jake called Tom on the following Monday about his recent staffing experience and awareness. He told him he was crystal clear he should be facilitating in the San Francisco advanced-level seminar. He asked Tom if he would consider training him for such a position. Tom's reaction to Jake's request was what he wanted but not what he expected. Tom said the board of directors and he had decided the previous week to search for someone to train. He suggested Jake should come to the next three seminars, and they would check him out, and he could determine if he wanted to be trained during that time. Jake was ecstatic. He was on the path of the personal transformation he wanted.

Jake attended the next seminar with Tom and his organization, filled with tremendous passion and hope for his future. Anything Dan asked of him, he jumped at the opportunity. Jake had been a problem solver his entire life, so he was the first to come up with a solution. It seemed nothing rattled him when it came to creating solutions. At the end of the weeklong seminar, Dan approached Jake and told him to be prepared to present at the next seminar the following month.

It was what he wanted to hear, but what would he be presenting? Dan said he would email Jake some notes to work with, and he expected Jake would be prepared. Jake was flying high when he returned home and shared the news with Grace. He had dreamed of this moment and would spend every minute preparing for it.

Over the next weeks, Jake prepared a presentation for the next seminar, but he was denied the opportunity when it came time to present. It seemed Dan wasn't willing to give up his time in front of the room, and Jake and the other facilitators-in-training had to compete for what little time there was. Though it was frustrating for everyone, Jake continued to prepare, transcribing recordings and practicing his presentations.

It was almost a year before Dan started spending less time in front of the room. Jake heard from Tom that he wanted the training process to speed up as he had more important matters for Dan to address. Not long after, Jake was in front of the room, fulfilling his dream. He was presenting lectures, facilitating experiential modules, and processing the participants through their journey. He couldn't be happier and wanted to transform himself and others as much as possible.

However, it wasn't all fun and games. Ahead of Jake in training was Teresa. She had managed to make her way into the owner's inner circle. She had his ear and was committed to taking Dan's place and becoming the lead facilitator for the seminar, which meant she would soon be responsible for the remainder of Jake's training.

The two of them created, what Jake thought, a close relationship. Jake was much older, and she treated him as a father figure in her life. She had experienced a lot of childhood trauma and didn't have the support of her father at the time. She, too, felt abandoned and held onto a lot of anger toward her father. In the line of fire, Teresa's anger would manifest at times, including when Jake would complete a presentation and return to his seat, where she would grill him about what she had observed. It was painful for Jake to hear her words, as his superiors had always encouraged him. It was as though she was deconstructing him with her critical observations.

There were also times when Jake and his new boss had fun and laughed about their personal experiences, both in the room and with their families. It seemed to Jake his boss had two extreme personalities: one was giving and loving, and one was angry and overly critical. It was impossible to know which one would show up at the seminar or when during the seminar, she would shift personalities. The other facilitators-in-training had similar experiences with her and would vent with Jake.

The training process began to slow down a great deal. Teresa had control over the seminar, and she wanted to spend as much time as possible in front of the room, working with the participants. Teresa wasn't giving the trainees much time in front of the room to practice.

Jake's competition was Sean, who, coincidently, was the same man who he had argued with during the Game of Life in his first three-day seminar. He was the man who had urged the other participants in his group to shut him up. He had been hired by the V.P. of sales as an inside salesperson a year earlier. Although he did his job well, his boss berated and criticized his every action. He finally had enough and requested to be transferred to the seminar team where Jake was training. Sean and Jake spent a great deal of time together and became allies in their training.

For over three years, Sean and Jake attended every seminar and submitted themselves to the training process the lead facilitator had created. It was a combination of tearing down everything they did, followed by pouring out love for them. They both wanted everything they could get from the training, so they kept showing up.

To his credit, Jake was good at handling the seminar's logistics, but he fell for the trap of *doing* tasks versus *being* authentic. As a facilitator, it was critical to show up in the right state of being. The participants connected with authenticity and vulnerability but rejected fear and intimidation. Jake's transformation was producing results, both for him and the company. He became an effective enroller, persuading the participants to sign up for the next level seminar.

Soon, the owners of the company were noticing Jake's facilitation team. They received notable recognition and additional bonuses at every corporate meeting. His team operated as one, so much so, only the lead facilitator was acknowledged for the leadership she provided. She had demanded any ideas or suggestions that produced results became the team's and not any one person's accomplishments.

However, Jake did not believe she operated under those rules. Often, Jake would suggest a change and later learn the lead facilitator would get all the credit for presenting the change to the owners. Over time, it became glaringly clear to Jake and the others this was not by accident but intentional. She was inching her way deeper and deeper into the inner circle of the company. Jake had seen this occur before during his earlier career in wood products. She intended to become one of the executives, even if it meant someone had to go from the team.

Time passed quickly for Jake in his training, and the day came for him to prove himself. His boss was expecting a child and was at the point she no longer could be in the room facilitating. For all he had been through, Jake was finally allowed to shine. The next seminar would be his debut, and he would take the role of lead facilitator. He would command the room, along with all the great results, or lack thereof. Jake knew he was deserving of this opportunity, and at the same time, he felt humbled the company was giving him so much trust. He wouldn't let them down, and he would make sure the participants and volunteer staff created a week they would talk about for years to come.

The seminar was well scripted when it came to the experiential learning modules and exercises but was a book with blank pages when it came to working with people. Emotional, physical, and mental safety were critical for the seminar's success, and Jake and the team had mastered those elements of the seminar.

The volunteer staff arrived a day early to prepare for supporting the new participants throughout the week. The prep work included setting up the room and participating in a staff meeting, where each member would undergo another transforming experience. To have an excellent context in which safety was the foundation, the staff would learn what context, in the seminar room, meant and their role in holding it. For most, this was a new concept and not easily understood. Jake worked with each staff member to drill down and expose what they wanted in life and why they hadn't created their desires.

The importance of the process meant the difference between creating extraordinary or ordinary results. The staff was eager to participate though their internal resistance showed up, which Jake helped them overcome. One at a time, Jake walked each staff member through a process where they created a new revelation and breakthrough. It would take a full day for the staff to come together, own the room, and learn their roles. The staff meeting prepared them for a wide range of possible human behavior scenarios, but they were instructed not to expect any person to act in any way.

It wouldn't be until the seminar was underway that their staff training kicked in, and they saw up close and personal how they each impacted the seminar and participants. Some staff would be responsible for multiple job duties, while others had only one. A chief of staff was responsible for the staff's state and the room's condition, with the producer overseeing it all. From keeping time, opening doors, positioning chairs, placing posters on the walls, working the resource table, creating posters, and playing music, the staff needed to function like a well-oiled machine. The participants deserved an excellent experience, and Jake's future depended not only on his results but also on those of the staff and his facilitation team.

With the support of his backup facilitator, producer, and staff, Jake led the team with authenticity, integrity, vulnerability, and courage. His transformation was also benefiting him as a leader. The new team of participants connected with him and his support team. They became vulnerable, shared their wounded hearts, and entrusted him and his team with their lives.

The team wouldn't learn until the last moments of the seminar they had been part of Jake's début as a lead facilitator. Sean disclosed the news to the team as they made their final comments in closing the seminar.

Jake and his team had done a flawless job, so not a single member of the new team had any idea it was his first time as the lead facilitator. One by one, the departing team members approached Jake and shared their gratitude for all he had done to help them overcome and break through their obstacles. Their words became new evidence that Jake had indeed transformed and was a man driven to support others in their journey.

The only way the company and his boss measured the results of any seminar was in the numbers. How many people did he enroll in the next level seminar? Though it was his first time as the lead facilitator, Jake and his team enrolled most of the new participants along with some of the staff into the next level seminar. His moment of truth had been realized, and Jake couldn't be happier.

LOOKING BACK:

For the first time in his life, Jake owned his results. His victim and scarcity mindsets were being overpowered by his new thinking of possibilities and abundance. He was willing to take risks and be in a relationship. He exposed his heart, knowing it could be crushed. His transformative moments had greater power than his childhood wounding, and he felt like there was nothing he couldn't create when he was crystal clear and committed.

Calling Tom proved to be an example of being clear with what he wanted to create going forward. Tom's quick response and invitation for Jake to step into a trainee's role had increased his confidence and were what he needed in his life. Jake began his training without knowing there were already two people ahead of him. Within the year, a fourth person would enter the scene, which slowed Jake's training significantly. The first two were women, one holding the position of producer and the other holding the second facilitator's position. The latter would become Jake's trainer and view him as her father figure. At first, he didn't see the harm in allowing her to view him this way, but in time, he would regret his decision.

Here is the tool taught to participants to use when one is faced with negative emotional issues, such as divorce—disappointments, betrayal, abandonment, death—and other matters of the heart. It is a process of *reframing* our negative emotional events.

The steps in the process are:

1. Write the negative event on the left side of a page.

2. Write what you made the event *mean* about you on the right side of the page, along with the narrative you created and have been telling.

3. On a different sheet, rewrite the same event again on the left side.

4. Write out a different, positive interpretation on the right side, along with a new narrative that might serve you better.

5. Compare the two interpretations and narratives and decide which will best serve you in creating greater success in your life.

6. Tear off the strip of paper with the ineffective interpretation and rip it into pieces and either burn it or throw it into the trash.

The symbolism of discarding the ineffective interpretation is important because you now have a new and effective interpretation to replace the old interpretation when it shows itself.

In Jake's experience, he used this kind of reframing to process through his abandonment issues. In his child's mind, being abandoned meant he was unlovable. Here we see the event—his father abandoning him—and his interpretation—what he made it mean about him. He must be unlovable. With these two pieces, he created a narrative in his unconscious mind to support his interpretation.

None of this happens in the conscious mind but in the unconscious mind. Jake's emotions and feelings allowed his subconscious to connect both the event of abandonment and his interpretation of being unlovable. Instantly, any abandonment experience, such as being fired, lack of intimacy with his spouse, or his child getting married and moving away, would include the same interpretation. Why? Because every human has an innate need to *be right*. To be right isn't something one invents or needs to practice. Being right is deep-rooted in our unconsciousness and is displayed when we are justifying or rationalizing our position.

Although Jake's father was an alcoholic and left home for months at a time, he was also a WWII veteran with medals for his heroic service and sacrifice. Before he went to war, he was a completely different man.

Jake *decided* deep within his father's being, that man existed but didn't know how to overcome himself. In Jake's reframing process, he *chose* to believe his father loved him so much he did what it took to be removed from his life so other men could enter in and mentor him. Five different men had a great deal of influence over him and taught him what it meant to be a man of integrity. The skills these men taught him were invaluable throughout his career. Though he struggled for 25 years to understand his in-laws' context of love for the family when his upbringing was the opposite, he eventually overcame his fixed mindset and learned to love himself and others.

On the next page is the exercise mentioned for reframing negative life experiences. You can list several types of experiences with your interpretation of what each means about you. Follow the exercise steps and see if the reframing of such events into a *positive interpretation* offers more support. After all, you created the original interpretation, which hasn't served you well. You have nothing to lose in creating a positive interpretation which may result in a new narrative to serve you better. Make those new narratives the foundation from which you choose to be right about your life and all the results you produce.

REFRAMING NEGATIVE LIFE EXPERIENCES

First Page	Step 1	Step 2
NAME THE EVENT	OLD INTERPRETATION
Abandoned	I am unlovable
	OLD NARRATIVE
	People can't be trusted to love and protect me so I won't love, trust or honor anyone that I am in relationship with.

Second Page	Step 3	Step 4
RECORD THE SAME EVENT	NEW INTERPRETATION
Abandoned	Dad loved me and he knew, deep down, that his addiction and mental state prevented him from being an effective father.
	NEW NARRATIVE
	Dad removed himself from my life in the hopes that one or more men could mentor me. Five men stood in the gap for my Dad and taught me what it meant to be a man and about masculinity and the responsibilities that came with being a man.
Step 5	Step 6
Compare the two interpretations and new narratives and decide which one serves you to create greater success in your life. Choose to keep that interpretation.	Tear off the old, ineffective, interpretation and narrative in Step 2 and either burn it or rip it to shreds and throw it in the trash.

YOUR INTROSPECTIVE CHALLENGE:

1. Describe one or more negative emotional experiences that when reframed would move you forward.

   _____

   _____

   _____

   _____

2. What is one thing you are committed to creating in your life?

   _____

   _____

   _____

   _____

3. What qualities did it take for Jake to fulfill his dream of being a Lead Facilitator?

   _____

   _____

   _____

   _____

4. What prices have you and others paid for your lack of commitment to your dream?

   _____

   _____

   _____

   _____

X

OBJECTS OR OBSTACLES

We do not see things as they are, we see them as we are.

—Anaïs Nin, *Seduction of the Minotaur*

How many times have you viewed another person as an obstacle standing in the way of your promotion? Did you feel a spouse, friend, or family member prevented you from realizing your dreams and goals? When they are honest with themselves, most people will tell you often they do see others as objects or obstacles in the way of the life they want to create. It isn't until we can see the humanity in others, we begin to see it in ourselves. And when we do, our world turns right side up, and what seems to be missing from our lives suddenly falls into place. It isn't because the right opportunities and people were never there, but rather, our limiting beliefs, decisions, and worldviews of who we think we are as a person blinds us. We can only see others as we see ourselves. If today were your last day on earth, whom would you want to contact to make things right?

———— ∞∞∞ ————

Jake was a child whose unconsciousness was in its formative period. His brain was developing its amygdala (emotional) neural pathways when he first learned he was viewed as an obstacle in his father's life. Though his parents' conversation wasn't meant for him to hear, he got the message loud and clear.

In anger, his father had verbally struck out at his mother to justify why he had not been the husband and father the family needed. "You and those damn kids have been a ball and chain around my neck our entire marriage."

Jake hadn't consciously thought about those words. He wasn't yet old enough to contemplate or process them and what his father was so poorly communicating. As his mother processed his father's words, the emotions he experienced would find their way into his subconscious and firmly take hold in his unconscious mind.

At first, she seemed to shut down, which lasted only a moment or two. Her anger spewed out in defense of her children and herself and filled the space surrounding them. The man whom she had dedicated her life to loving by putting up with his alcoholism, his running away for months at a time, and his building up debt greater than they could manage had declared her to be inhuman and of no value to him. To make matters worse, he included her children. Forgiving him again was out of the question. He had to go and go immediately. Jake was caught up in their emotions, terrified from the yelling between his parents, and he started to cry uncontrollably. Without having to think about it, he felt unlovable, worthless, and rejected. He believed he must be to blame for their fight and his mother's choice to run his father off.

Seeing his father walk across the floor to the front door was more than he could take. "Dad, come back! Come back, please!" he screamed. His words were ineffective, and his father kept walking. Standing in the open doorway, Jake again called out, "When will I see you again?"

"It's up to your mother" was his father's retort.

Jake stood in the doorway as his father drove away and until the car was out of sight.

Being human means you will get wounded physically, emotionally, and mentally many times in your life. How you respond to these wounds largely determines your destiny. Although our mistakes do not define us, we are responsible for how we respond to everything life brings our way. Unaware of how he was being affected by his father's departure, Jake began to create himself as an independent, guarded, untrusting, and unlovable man. Each of these traits was burned into his unconscious mind by the emotions he felt and those he experienced from his mother the day he saw his father walk away.

He came to believe if you cannot trust your parents to care for and love you, no other person can be trusted. He experienced the intense pain of loss and fear, which pierced his heart so deeply he grew up guarding against letting anyone get close enough to wound him again. He didn't need to depend on anyone for his safety, love, or support. In his mind, he would walk through life alone and vowed to become more than either of his parents ever had.

At a young age, Jake vowed if he ever married, he would do whatever it took to stay married longer than his mother and father. Those words were spoken out loud, only days after his father left the family, as he stood at the curb where his father's car had been parked. He wasn't angry when he said those words. From a wounded heart, he was speaking intentionally, not knowing what his childhood vow would come to mean in his life.

Jake's spoken vow penetrated his subconscious and, like a planted seed, would germinate over time. His decisions and worldviews were developing from it. With each large and small negative emotional experience, his heart became more hardened. People who stood between what he wanted and himself became obstacles for him to overcome. Anyone wishing to get close had to prove to him they trusted him unconditionally. He shut down emotionally and withdrew into his world.

Depression in his birth family was common, and he was not immune. He would often slip into a dark depression where he wouldn't speak to anyone for long periods. Days, weeks, and months passed without him having any semblance of a social conversation. Often, Grace would ask, "Why don't you talk to me?" His silence was a fuel that fed every argument between them. He knew something was wrong, but as an independent man, he couldn't find the courage to seek out help.

During his depressed state, Jake experienced a sense of floating out of and above his body. He was keenly aware of his state of being and wanted to cry out to this suffering man. "Wake up, wake up!" he heard in his mind. But the words would not cross his lips. So, he did what he had always done: he poured more of himself into his work. Working as much as 100 hours a week numbed the pain he was experiencing and provided a hiding place where he felt in control and safe.

The intensity of his facilitation training increased as the demand for seminars and corporate training increased. Flying out on Sunday afternoon provided him time to arrive in San Francisco and settle in for a Monday training session with his new boss, Teresa, and the rest of the facilitation team. Together, they practiced presenting the lecture as a lead-in for an exercise. Although he had debuted his abilities, creating great results, his boss seemed to expect perfection. Her critique targeted him more and more, humiliating him, both in practice and in the seminar room, with the participants looking on. It wasn't uncommon for one or more of the participants to approach him at the end of the seminar and express their frustration with his boss for how she treated him. Like Jake, they were embarrassed to witness such treatment and wanted him to know they gained much from his presentations.

Tom's company was experiencing rapid growth, and the demand for public and corporate seminars required more and more of Jake's time. With seminars across the nation, Canada, Australia, and Europe, the demand for his time to facilitate increased exponentially.

Some months, he would facilitate in two to three weeklong seminars back-to-back. After a week in San Francisco, the team would fly to Australia's Gold Coast for another week, then back to San Francisco for a week before he would fly home. It was common for the team to work up to one 115 hours during these weeks. The international flights were long, but when they landed, the focus was on getting ready for the staff training the next day. All the logistical items and staff training would take place the day leading up to the seminar's opening.

⸻ ∞ ⸻

Our childhood's limiting decisions, beliefs, and worldviews filter how we view each other and the world at large. Our secrets must mean we are different somehow. A young boy who is repeatedly told he will never amount to anything or was never wanted by his parents comes to believe he is different than the other boys around him. He will lack courage, confidence, and ambition. His life will be wrought with failures, broken relationships, financial loss, and betrayal. A young girl who never experiences her importance to her father comes to believe she isn't worth fighting for and has no value. She will seek these things, and more, from other boys and men who show any interest in her. Some will act out in self-harming ways, such as cutting, promiscuity, and drug and alcohol use. Her life, too, may be one of broken relationships, unwanted pregnancies, financial struggles, and feelings of unworthiness.

Each put on a masquerade to imply they have everything figured out. But on the inside, they are a wreck. The energy used to hide their secret wounds takes away from the energy they need for creating the life they want. Likely, friends don't know of the wounds, the kind never to be exposed to family. The weight of the pain is carried throughout their lives and projected into each relationship created. Their pose works for them for a while. But, as soon as a trigger event occurs, all pain comes spewing out, and those who have been important to them become objects and are now the recipients of the rage and pain. Jake saw this happen over and over between his parents.

He and Grace developed a similar kind of relationship but without the physical abuse he had witnessed so often as a child. He didn't have any idea what he wanted to create, so he had buckled under the demands of providing for his family.

Living life from a *victim mindset* prevents a person from seeing all the possibilities and opportunities around them. What they see are the obstacles and objects that stand in the way of their safety and what they want to create. Jake's life had been created and lived from such a mindset. During one of his walkthroughs of the manufacturing plant, one of the employees engaged him in conversation. She was asking about his aspirations and how he planned to realize them. He surprised the employee with his response. He planned to overcome all obstacles that stood between him and his goals even if it meant going over, around, or through the people who stood in his way. He saw himself separate from everyone else, and they were an opposing force he would overcome. In his victim view, they were objects and obstacles in his path of success.

Imagine the loss a man or woman like this is creating in his or her life over and over. He or she doesn't have close personal relationships, business relations are surface, and production is the priority. He or she may perform at a high level but from chance, circumstance, and fear. The fear of being hurt drives this kind of person so hard the wake of injuries to others is obvious to everyone but him or herself. Life's events are responded to from victim thinking. In other words, life is being done to him or her versus him or her creating life from choice and commitment.

This type of person does not understand what it means to take responsibility for his or her life. The victim worldview isn't filled with solutions for this person but, rather, the same old tired options of remaining stuck—feeling unworthy, living in denial, hiding out, feeling unaccomplished, lacking financial resources, being untrusting of others, feeling afraid to ask for support—and complaining about everyone else and their success.

How do you know if you operate from a *victim mindset?* Like a fish removed from the water it lives in, the only way to know is to step outside that mindset and examine it from a different viewpoint, the viewpoint known as *responsible.* I am not speaking of fault or blame. If you believe responsibility is all about fault, you are operating in a victim mindset, and your worldviews are anchored from that viewpoint. These two viewpoints are like looking at two sides of a coin. Regardless of the side of the coin you are looking at, it remains a coin.

Take, for example, the 1974 U.S. minted dollar coin. On the obverse side, there is an image of a man, Dwight D. Eisenhower, 34th president of the U.S. The date, 1974, is below the image; the words, "In God We Trust," are to the left of the image, and the word, "LIBERTY," is wrapped around the top of the coin. The coin appears to be made of silver overlaid on a copper interior with ridges around the coin's edge. These are specifics you would see from this viewpoint.

By Brandon Grossardt for the photograph; Frank Gasparro for the coin design. - Actual coin., Public Domain, https://commons.wikimedia.org/w/index. php?curid=26566351

If at the same time, another person was looking at the reverse side of the coin, they would see completely different images. In the center, an eagle in flight with olive branches in its talons is the focal point. Below the eagle are the words, "ONE DOLLAR," wrapped at the top of the coin are the words, "UNITED STATES OF AMERICA," with the words, "*E Pluribus Unum,*" below. Thirteen stars, representing the original thirteen colonies, are stamped into the coin and representing the Apollo 11 moon landing is the insignia designed by Michael Collins.

By Brandon Grossardt for the photograph; Frank Gasparro for the coin design. - Actual coin., Public Domain, https://commons.wikimedia.org/w/index. php?curid=26566351

Two people looking at the same coin from two different viewpoints would believe they are right as they described what they are seeing. And they would be right. Their viewpoints are their experience and precisely what they are seeing. What if one side of the coin is called victim, and the other side responsible?

Recall a negative emotional experience from your past and describe the experience from the victim viewpoint out loud, standing in front of a mirror, to yourself or in-person to a friend. Feel the emotions of the time and express the words you might have used both in tone and energy. If you were trying to convince another person you were victimized, you might need to go back in time and bring forth evidence that supports your narrative. The more dramatic you describe the experience of the event, the more convincing you'll be. You might even breakdown and cry to dramatize being victimized. Remember, this is the viewpoint of the victim. If you told a convincing narrative, you and your friend would believe you were victimized.

Telling the exact same narrative from the responsible viewpoint will create a different result. Give it a try, speaking out loud to yourself or a friend but, this time, use the phrase, "I chose," with each sentence. When expressing a responsible narrative, this phrase, "I chose," empowers where the victim viewpoint disempowers. Responsible means you deal with only the facts, without drama, shame, blame, or guilt. *I chose* will empower you to see the options and possibilities available you cannot see when in the victim mindset. Start earlier, days, weeks, or months before the event, and look at all the choices you made that led up to the event. Notice any intuitive urging you may have ignored.

Here is where the value of this exercise becomes glaringly apparent. With every choice we make, there are costs and rewards. Take a piece of paper and write "VICTIM" at the top. Begin to list all the rewards you can think of coming from the victim mindset.

- You will gain sympathy from others.
- You get to play life safe.
- There's no need to be responsible for your results.

- You get to be right.
- Others take care of your needs.
- You protect your image.
- You feel entitled.

The list could go on and on, but you get the gist of this part of the exercise. Remember, *victim* means that life is being done to you and therefore guides your experience.

Take another sheet of paper and write "RESPONSIBLE" across the top. Now, list as many of the rewards you can think of when you told your story from this viewpoint. They might include:

- Greater clarity
- More control
- Greater understanding of the event
- A sense of freedom
- Empowerment
- More accepting
- Ready to forgive

This list, too, could be much longer. As you review the two lists, which viewpoint would move you forward? Of course, it is the responsible viewpoint. When you live life from a victim viewpoint, there aren't any solutions to move forward. From responsible, however, there are solutions everywhere for you.

Growing up in a family culture of victimhood, Jake lived half his life believing the world owed him. As a child, his mother went on welfare when she couldn't work due to illness. The welfare system provided $50 per month to pay rent and put food on the table. He felt like he had to work to help his mother, so he worked after school and weekends. From his earliest memories, he worked versus everything boys his age were doing. Shifting his mindset to responsible took a deeper dive into his core beliefs and owning them because he believed he was a victim didn't make it true. He realized his parents' beliefs had been incorporated into his life, were harmful, and didn't support what he wanted and who he wanted to become.

Victimhood is all around us. Take a walk down any street in a major city and notice how the victim mindset is operating in the population. Listen to the conversations in a restaurant. It isn't only there. It is on the nightly news, in the newspapers, and posted on social media platforms, all filled with victim stories. Everyone, at one time or another, takes on the victim mindset. We live in painful and negative experiences so we can play the victim. For clarity, I am not saying a child creates being molested or harmed in any way. I'm saying, at an unconscious level, we will make choices that put us at the wrong place and time with people who can cause us harm. As adults, how we choose to respond to our childhood trauma determines which mindset we choose.

Or we may choose to drive recklessly and cause a wreck where we and others are injured. An abused person often chooses new relationships to satisfy their unconscious programming to be right: that men or women will hurt you. Suppose during your formative years, love in your family looked like screaming, hitting, shutting down, running away, abuse, and more. You may unconsciously seek those attributes in your close relationships so you *feel* loved. Go back and review the rewards in your VICTIM list.

But what about the costs we pay for playing the victim? What are they? Everything and more you listed on the RESPONSIBLE page! There is no room for excuses and justification, poor performance, procrastinating, blaming others, and playing it safe. You give up, blaming yourself as well.

One viewpoint or the other isn't necessarily true, right, or wrong. Each one supports us in creating different experiences and possibilities or the lack thereof. You have the power to choose which viewpoint you will live from going forward. Accepting to be 100% responsible for the results you create gives you freedom. All human's default position is victim, whether you consciously choose it or not. Being robbed, raped, abused, betrayed, abandoned, and fired are all instances that can make us feel victimized. Choosing to live life as a victim, because of these kinds of events, robs us of the passion and purpose we are meant to live. Make a choice today to shift from victim to responsible and enjoy more freedom and liberty.

—⊗∞⊗—

LOOKING BACK:

Once Jake had owned he was an obstacle in his father's mind, he began to see everyone else the same. Anyone who stood between him creating safety for himself and his family paid the price. At times, he was harsh with his family and his employees. Those he dealt with felt his iron hand and rigid approach and principles. The sawmill employees, supervisors, loggers, truck drivers, longshoremen, union stewards, and union business secretaries were all subject to his ways. He had developed *my way or the highway* attitude. For him, it was fall in line or leave.

However, when the same was done to him, he was devastated. His world crumbled around him, and he felt *victimized*, once again. His unwillingness to trust others was foundational in his lack of close friends and business relations. This became all too apparent when he played the Game of Life when he realized he had never trusted anyone, including himself, completely. He was a victim of his childhood and carried that into his adult life. Victims surrounded him, and he felt he could control them. Every negative emotional event was rooted in his emotions and feelings of being abandoned, betrayed, and victimized. He was either unaware of how he was interpreting these events or unwilling to view them from a different perspective, the perspective of responsible. From the responsible viewpoint, there were many solutions from which to choose. He believed he was responsible but living in his victim view meant *it* was his fault, or he was to blame. This viewpoint brought with it shame and guilt. Both of which he had taken ownership of when his mother explained his father had never wanted children in the first place. She reinforced this during every visit he made to her home as an adult. During one such visit, feeling the pain of her words, he had blurted out, "You both wanted something because you birthed nine children and had six miscarriages."

When Jake finally realized how his worldviews had gripped his mind, he felt like a broken man. How could he have been so blinded, so judgmental, and so angry? His understanding of how he had a choice in the way he responded to life's circumstances expanded greatly.

His mind began to open, and he felt filled with a love of self and others he'd never experienced. It was overwhelming and overflowing, pouring out to others but never emptying. Joy and passion for life were burning hot inside him, and he wanted to share that with everyone who crossed his path. Jake wasn't only changing. He was transforming into the man he was meant to be. He had a future he would create and choose to be responsible for every result he manifested in his life.

YOUR INTROSPECTIVE CHALLENGE:

1. In what ways have you viewed others as objects or obstacles standing in your way?

   _____

   _____

   _____

   _____

2. What kind of relationship have you created with these people?

   _____

   _____

   _____

   _____

3. From the victim mindset, what important sacrifices did you make?

   _____

   _____

   _____

   _____

4. From the responsible mindset, what is one quality choice you can make today to move forward?

   _____

   _____

   _____

   _____

XI

OPPORTUNITIES & POSSIBILITIES

*The greatest burden a child must bear is the unlived life
of its parents.*

—Carl Jung

I often ask people in my seminars, "What do you want to create?" They answer something along these lines: "I have no idea," or "I stopped dreaming a long time ago." Hearing these responses is heartbreaking because they became a dead man walking long ago and gave up on their dreams and aspirations. Each has settled for whatever came their way and gave up on the life they were meant to live.

They've begun to operate in the shadows, hoping no one would learn of their secret wounds. They live in and operate from a state of denial. Opportunities and possibilities surround them, but fearing they will fail again, they play it safe and sit on the sidelines. And when they look back, they realize they have become their parents in so many ways. How is it possible to shift our thinking? Is it possible to transform our thinking and respond to life differently?

Jake worked with thousands of people of many races and cultures and facilitated transformational seminars across the globe for eighteen years. He discovered most people stop dreaming and imagining they have the power to create significant results in their life around the ages of 13 to 21. Some children may stop dreaming earlier, especially where there is a lot of drama and trauma in the home, and their focus is on survival.

These are the years famed marketing professor and sociologist, Morris Massey, called the socialization years.[6] Individuals seem to feel they are too old to be a child and know, until age 18, they are too young to be considered an adult. They are seeking their place in society and questioning who they are. The imprinting years between birth and age seven and the modeling years between seven and 13, are behind them, and they feel clumsy and out of place when it comes to socialization. Massey believed and taught, "We are largely influenced by our peers. As we develop as individuals and look for ways to get away from the earlier programming, we naturally turn to people who seem more like us. Other influences at these ages include the media, especially those parts that seem to resonate with the values of our peer groups."[7]

"If money and time were not an obstacle, what would you want to create?" Jake asked his audience.

Moments of silence passed before one brave soul spoke up. "I want to buy a house!"

Then, another person chimed in, "I want to double my income."

Another shouted, "I want to get my degree."

Another said, "I want to travel."

And another shouted, "I want to start my own business."

Quickly, he wrote each possibility on the board. Finally, stepping back and reading through the list, he turned and asked the crowd, "If these are your dreams, your goals, then why don't you already have them?"

"Fear," someone called out.

"I don't know what to do to get started," said another.

"I'm afraid of what my family might say," said another.

Looking over the audience, he agreed all their answers were true, at least to some degree. But he had another point of view. "I think it's because humans are a lot like dogs." The audience laughed. "It's true, and we are like dogs. If you take your dog and put a bowl of bones on the opposite side of the room and a bowl of steak beside the bones and turn your dog loose, which bowl will your dog choose?

"The steak, of course!" someone called out.

"That's right," he said. "Dogs will go for the steak this time, next time, and every time because they like steak better. But they will settle for the bones. My questions for you: 'What bones are you settling for in your life?' Is it an okay marriage instead of a spectacular marriage? Is it a job you hate, but you stick with because it pays the bills? Are you in an unhealthy state of being because you aren't motivated to do something about it? Have you not realized your dreams and goals because of some excuse you have come to believe about who you are and your value?"

He sensed he was hitting a nerve with every statement and question he issued. Jake had sat in their place when he was first introduced to the concepts he presented to them. He knew what it felt like to settle for little when he was in survival mode. He had lived through the loss of jobs, believing he didn't have choices, wanting more but never knowing where or how to start.

His audience members were a microcosm of people like him, and the real world was filled with them. There was urgency in reaching them because in the room were marriages on the verge of divorce, business owners looking for ways to stay open, students about to drop out of college, individuals suffering from depression, and worse, those dealing with suicidal ideation. Time was of the essence, and he had an important and life-transforming message to deliver.

⚉

"Let me tell you something about why we have all settled, at some time or other, in our lives. Pay close attention! I'm about to open your minds to greater possibilities: your dreams, goals, and more. Each of us is made up of three levels of being: our conscious, subconscious, and what I have identified for me, God. You may choose to use universal power, higher power, or superconscious. The fact is each person is created this way.

"Our first level of being is our consciousness used for thinking—decision-making, contemplation, awareness, sensations, feelings, memories, fantasies, and more. For a great number of us, we spend most of our awakened state in our conscious mind. With increases in technology, this time has become exponentially greater. We are either on our phones, tablet, or computer, working in our jobs and businesses or watching TV. We create lists of things we want to get done in a day and lament over what we failed to accomplish, rather than celebrate what we did accomplish.

"The next level is our subconscious mind. Within our subconscious are suppressed urges—feelings, emotions, knowledge, programming—and thoughts. Many of the things we learn are stored in our subconscious. They can be quickly brought into our consciousness when needed.

> "Sometimes, our unconscious is revealed in our dreams."
> —Sigmund Freud and Tipitaka

"Sometimes, our unconscious is revealed in our dreams, as written in, *Evaluating the Unconscious Dream*, between Sigmund Freud and the Buddhist Tipitaka.[8] Haven't you ever gone to bed with a problem you couldn't solve, then awakened with a solution to the problem fresh in your mind? That's because your subconscious has a storehouse of knowledge and information your consciousness doesn't have and shouldn't be bothered with all the time.

"If you were working out a mathematical problem, you would automatically draw upon your subconscious mind to provide you with the formula and steps to get to the answer. Who has ever gone to bed knowing you had to awaken at 5:00 a.m. but didn't set the alarm and awoke on time or within a minute or two of the time? That happens because our subconscious mind is working for us 100% of the time. Every pattern for creating, problem-solving, inventing, and more, which you have ever been exposed to, reside in your subconscious and are available to be called forth when needed. Some might say our connectedness to each other and God provides unlimited resources. In other words, you have a supercomputer at your conscious disposal.

"The third level of being is our connection to our infinite power or what I call God. Wisdom comes from this third level. Our moral compass and values come from this level of being. When all three levels of being are in alignment, we become more powerful than we can imagine. Those dreams and goals seem impossible to realize, become manifest when we are aligned and use all three levels for creating. Everyone has created results this way. But most people are unaware of how or what they did to create their desired results. Some people have become proficient and have created great wealth and influence using all three levels of their being, consistently.

"In Napoleon Hill's book, *Think and Grow Rich*, Hill speaks of the Mastermind effect; 'No two minds ever come together without thereby creating a third, invisible, intangible force, which may be likened to a third mind,' also known as, the Mastermind.[9] Hill's writings on this subject intended to help people come together in groups and share their knowledge, talents, skills, and more to create more of their wants. Collaborating with others, who are also aligning their own three levels of being, Hill believed each person could tap into the third mind, the Mastermind. This resulted in the individuals' success, and the group creating more of an environment to achieve their goals."

Jake was on a roll and with great excitement, as he was looking forward to the crescendo, a formula for creating results when you have no idea what to do. His mentor had taught him this years earlier. He used this formula regularly, even though, in the beginning, he didn't fully understand its power. With practice, he and Grace had created some seemingly impossible results in their marriage and business. Even his mentor had admitted it took him five years before he fully grasped the power of the formula, which he had learned from his mentor.

Jake drew a circle on the board. He drew a much larger circle below it and connected each with a straight line. Below he drew a half-circle and connected it to the second circle with another straight line. "The three images represent your different levels of being," he said. Based on what he had previously presented, he continued his lecture by demonstrating the conscious mind's (head) connection with the subconscious (heart) and God, or the superconscious, universal power, higher power. The connecting lines indicated the alignment of the three levels. He did a quick review of what each level is responsible for, stressing that if they remembered anything, he wanted them to remember the number he was about to write on the board.

In large red letters, Jake wrote out 99%. That was the percentage of all decisions made by our subconscious. "We don't consciously make them," he added. "We operate in automatic much of the time. Most of us drive a car and have experienced arriving at our destination and realized we don't remember much of our surroundings along the way. We were daydreaming and not focused, but our subconscious mind knew the way and guided us safely.

"If I asked each of you, 'Did you decide to be here?' what would you say? Yes, of course, I decided to come here. My butt's in the chair. You think you made that decision, but I suggest something else decided for you. Do you know people who said they would come to this gathering, but they didn't show up?"

"Yes, I was supposed to meet two of my friends here," responded one of the attendees.

"I bet if we called them to check-in and make sure they were safe, they'd say something like 'I was too tired after work,' or 'I decided I didn't need what was going to be offered,' or 'My life is great—I wouldn't change a thing.' It looks as though they decided not to come, but I'm suggesting something else decided. I'm suggesting you aren't deciding to prospect or how to prospect if you are in sales. If you're married, you didn't pick your spouse. You aren't choosing when or how to be intimate.

"Those with children, would you like to have a more meaningful relationship with them? If you say yes, then you aren't deciding how that looks, or you'd already have that kind of relationship. By a show of hands, who here is making less money than they want to make? If you raised your hand, you made my point for me. If you were deciding how much money you make, you'd pick a larger salary. What I'm saying is you are not in control. Something else is. We want to believe we are in control, but we are not. I'm not saying you have to like my point, but can you see, if this is true, it's why you don't create the results you say you want?"

Jake was amazed at his power of persuasion.

"So, what is the thing that controls our self-limiting decisions, beliefs, and worldviews? If you have lenses that filter everything you take in, which by the way, is some 2.6 million bits of information per second, what is powerful enough to process all that data? I suggest it is our subconscious mind. Consciously, we are only able to process about 126 bits of data per second. The rest is filtered out by deletion, distortion, and generalizing. Being born into a culture of poverty, negativity, and scarcity is almost like coming out of the womb with lenses that prevent you from seeing possibilities. For instance, if my lenses were green, all my worldviews would be filtered through green lenses. Could I ever see anything without believing it was green? Could you convince me, persuade me, threaten me, or force me to see any color but green? No, of course not!

"When our core beliefs and worldviews are anchored with false or incomplete evidence, the only way to shift our thinking is to have revelations where we discover these lenses. How do you have such revelations, you might ask? By encountering a significant emotional event and doing your detective work to discover why you believe what you do. By detective work, I'm referring to noticing your behavior and feelings, which are part of your unconscious programming. The ancient text, 'As a man or woman thinketh in their heart, so are they,' refers to the subconscious mind, your supercomputer for creating and solving problems. If you believe all men or women can't be trusted, ask yourself why. If you believe money is evil, ask yourself why. If you believe you can't be a good Christian and have financial wealth, ask yourself why. If you believe yourself to be unworthy, ask why. As you examine each of your core beliefs, take note of your feelings and behaviors that show up. Asking another person to tell you what they notice about you and what you are saying is a good way to validate your learning."

Jake continued, "The fact is each of us has hundreds, if not thousands, of these kinds of lenses that we filter information through. And, if your lenses are self-limiting, no matter the effort, desire, wish, or hope you have for a certain goal, the odds of you achieving that goal are monumentally slim. Should you realize your goal, you will likely sabotage yourself, so you lose that thing you managed to create. I call it being a lottery winner. We all know the stories of men and women who have won the lottery, and in one, two, or three years, they are right back at the status of life they were living or, for some, below and worse off financially.

"The good news is we each have the power to change our thinking, our self-limiting beliefs, and worldviews at our subconscious level."

———— ∞∞∞ ————

His audience was now ready to receive a gift that would support them in creating greater goals and visions when integrated into their subconscious mind. His first mentor in personal development, Tom, had passed a similar formula on to Jake in his early training days. Through the years, Jake had learned many people didn't fully understand the original formula because Tom used the word intention as part of the formula. Intention is more like having a wish for something. Even Tom realized the word intention didn't carry the energy needed, so he defined it as "your deepest commitment." Working with thousands of individuals and business leaders in goal-setting and achievement of those goals, Jake learned when people focused on their intention, many would fail to take the required action to realize their goal.

To provide his audiences with a tool they could integrate immediately, one that produced results no matter the circumstances, he revised the formula to commitment plus action equals results (C + A = R). He compared commitment to Napoleon Hill's definite purpose when in a mastermind with others while pledging, you would create a specific goal or outcome. When combined with taking persistent action, sometimes a sequence of small measurable steps toward the goal will help a person realize their desired results.

"Today, each of you will leave with the keys to your very own, new CAR!" He got a kick out of this statement because it reminded him of a couple of television shows where the contestant played some sort of game that had a new car as the prize. In this case, each person was invited to play in an experiential learning game to learn about Jake's formula, then put it into action.

"I'm looking for a volunteer, someone who is ready to step into leadership." In every room he had ever been in, he could hear a pin drop during the moments following that request, but someone always stepped forward and declared they were ready to be a leader.

To gain the value of the presentation, you would want to ask yourself a few questions. Remember, play detective by noticing your behaviors and feelings. Why didn't you step up, might be a question to ask? Some would answer, "I'm always the leader and wanted to give someone else the chance to step up." Another person might say, "I don't know what you are going to have us do." Or "I don't like to be the center of attention."

There are as many excuses for holding back as there are people in the room. The real question is, "Where else in my life do I do this same thing, and what are the prices others and I are paying for me playing it safe?"

When being radically honest, people reveal they have been humiliated in the past when they stepped forward to take leadership. As a child, they were never picked to be the leader and often were the last ones picked to be on a team. They didn't like the responsibility that came with being a leader because of being blamed or shamed for lack of expected results. The list is long. But it boils down to one thing: leadership begins with yourself. If you haven't learned how to be an effective leader of yourself, don't expect to lead others.

When a person takes him or herself on at this level and digs deep, they have an opportunity for both revelation and breakthrough. The discovery of what has held a person back can be life-transforming. Getting back to the one person who did step forward, let's explore what drove them to take the lead.

"What caused you to step forward and say, I'll do it?" Jake asked.

To the surprise of many, this person might respond he or she is ready to do and be more than ever before. He or she may feel stuck in life and know if they don't take a risk now, they might remain stuck for the next five years. The person might feel the environment is a safe place for them to practice leadership. On the job, opportunities have great risks, so they hold back and play it safe. Regardless of why someone steps forward, everyone could learn from each other.

To the surprise of many, this person might respond he or she is ready to do and be more than ever before. He or she may feel stuck in life and know if they don't take a risk now, they might remain stuck for the next five years. The person might feel the environment is a safe place for them to practice leadership. On the job, opportunities have great risks, so they hold back and play it safe. Regardless of why someone steps forward, everyone could learn from each other.

Jake began to cover the rules of the game. First and foremost was their safety. They were not to do anything that would put them in harm's way. They had a choice whether they participate or not. The game was an individual experience, so people would complete it by themselves. Except for the person in action, everyone else was his or her cheerleader. The game was played in the room they were all in now. Then, he told them the objective of this game.

"Each person will come to the front of the line and declare their goal to the audience. Once they make their declaration, they will cross the room, touch the wall, and return to the group. Returning to the group is as if they have realized their goal. The kind of goal or the time, which you believe it will take to realize the goal, is irrelevant in this experience. Once you touch the wall and return to the group, we will celebrate your accomplishment."

He created a context within which they could get glimpses of one or more of their lenses, limiting decisions, beliefs, and worldviews. Being in action would cause them to experience their bodies and not be thinking about what they were doing. They would behave very differently than their norm and begin to feel more than think. They were ready.

He brought the first person to the starting point and reminded them to declare their goal to the group. The person was a bit anxious at first, then declared she was going to create an extra $10,000 by the end of the year. She turned around and began to walk across the room. Reaching the other side, she touched the wall and turned around and stood still. Jake let a moment pass, then asked the group, "Based on the formula, $C + A = R$, what is she doing?"

"She is showing us her commitment," said one person.

"She is in action," said another.

He then asked, "Based on what is taking place at this moment, what part of the formula is she using?"

"Action!" someone called out.

"None of it!" said another. "She is standing still."

"Based on what is taking place in the room right now, what do we know about her?"

"She is committed to her goal."

After five or more minutes, a light bulb moment happened for the woman, and she began to walk back toward the group. As she crossed the starting point, the group cheered for her. Tears ran down her cheeks as people from the group hugged her and gave high-fives.

Jake approached her and asked why she was so emotional. She acknowledged once she got to the other side of the room, she didn't know what to do, so she stopped. Her mind raced as Jake was talking to the group about the formula. She didn't understand why he was so insistent on identifying what was happening when she was only standing there. Her light bulb moment was the realization that she had a behavior of jumping into things before she knew all the facts. That she over committed and ended up not getting most of her commitments accomplished. The clarity of her revelation caused her to start walking, so she completed the game.

This person's experience was typical of any person who would have taken the lead. Some would get partway back and stop, reporting they viewed Jake as an obstacle. They were waiting for his permission to continue. The person would confess they are continually seeking approval, whether at home with a spouse or at work with their boss or coworkers. Others would back up to the wall and freeze in their footprints, almost as though they were giving up on their goal. Later, they would share with the group that too many times they had bought into someone else's dream or goal and didn't have the passion for completing it. These people jumped from job to job, relationship to relationship, and church to church, expecting to be fulfilled by others' passion and purpose.

The first person had made it back safely, and it was time for each of them to create their experience. But before they could, Jake added in a few obstacles. First, because person number one had used walking to cross the room, no one could walk. If someone chose to hop, then no one that followed him or her could hop. Should another decide to run, running was out.

Before he could continue, a loud cry came from the crowd. "Stop! You're using all the ways we can cross the room."

The group began to reshape itself with people making their way as close to the front as possible. He reminded them if they weren't crossing, and they had to cross one at a time, the rest of them were cheering. And lastly, he added everyone had to use a new and unique way to cross the room, saying, "If someone tries to use a way that has already been used, the group is to make a sound to get their attention." That person would return to the front of the line and choose a different way to cross. The group agreed on the cheering noise they'd make would be the sound of a loud buzzer to stop the person.

This time, the wall on the other side of the room was the destination, and touching the wall represented realizing their goal. Person after person crossed the room. One would skip, another dance, another twirl, another crawled. Dozens of ways were used by the time everyone crossed. He would have them repeat this back and forth, crossing the room several times until one person stalled out at the front of the line. This would be a teaching moment for the group. As he often did, Jake asked the person if they were willing to be the teacher at the moment so the group could create maximum value. Not one person had ever said no.

He asked the group if they were willing to let this person represent them for the remainder of the exercise. As was the case in all his training, they all enthusiastically agreed. Jake was going to test this person's commitment. Not necessarily for the goal he or she had stated but, rather, their commitment in their life. This person and all those in the room were about to witness and experience a significant emotional event. This would be the kind of experience that had the power to cause a person to question his or her values programming. Such an experience was responsible for Jake's transformation of his character, self-limiting core beliefs, decisions, and worldviews—his lenses.

"In this next part of the game, your boss has declared that an austerity program is being implemented. For you, that means your hours and income are cut by 25%. Now, to cross the room, you are limited to using one arm and one leg only. GO!" The woman stood there for a moment, then sitting down, she used her leg to push her body across the room. The group cheered wildly for her as she stood and faced them. A wide grin appeared on her face as she internalized the acknowledgment.

"We're not finished yet," he said. "You have been given a dreaded pink slip; you will be terminated at the end of the week. The first pay cut caused you to use much of your savings, and you don't have any reserves. If you don't find a job and find it soon, you and your children will likely be on the streets. To represent the seriousness of this, cross the room without allowing any part of you or what you are wearing to touch the floor. Go!"

This time, the woman was stuck. A solution was not apparent whether she was imagining what it might look like to be homeless, or this scenario represented some aspect of her life. To increase the intensity, Jake added a count-down to her time, beginning within a week after she depleted her savings. Each day passed, with him announcing the number of days left. She was being pressed harder and harder to create a solution. The last few hours of the final day were ticking by, when, suddenly, she grabbed two books off the table, and using them as skis, she crossed the room with an excited group receiving her.

Tears ran down her face and the faces of many of the people in the group as well. She shared in her life she had faced circumstances that were as life-threatening as the scenario she experienced. Like this time, she froze, unable to see a way forward until there was a greater price to pay. It took a high level of fear of loss before becoming crystal clear about what she wanted before she saw solutions. At that moment, she could move forward, seemingly effortlessly.

Jake put the formula on the board, $C + A = R$, and asked the group, "What percent of commitment does it take to accomplish any goal?"

The responses ranged from 25, 30, 50, to 100 percent. "If any of that is true, then what percent of action does it take?" Again, the percentages were similar with a couple of variations. As they looked over the information on the board, he asked, "What percent equals results?"

The group seemed to agree that the correct answer was 100 percent. He turned to the woman who had represented the whole group and asked, "What part of the formula caused you to create a solution?"

Without hesitation, she responded, "It was the clarity I had for the goal I set. I suddenly knew I had to be 100% committed to my goal." She had experienced a significant emotional event, which almost instantly caused her to examine her values programming around commitment. Realizing her gut-level response to life had been casual, in many cases, she chose to shift her mindset and, in an instant, created the results that she wanted.

Addressing the group, Jake said the true formula is C = R. He explained an A for action was required, as in some sort of mechanism for accomplishing your goal, but commitment will always create a result. The key is you have to be crystal clear on your commitment, or only busyness or inactivity will be your result.

"When you are clear, your mechanism will appear. This formula will work for you 100% of the time. If you are producing less than what you say you are committed to, you need to examine your commitment. Why do you want a certain thing? What are the prices you and others will pay if you don't produce your desired results? To increase your commitment, do these three things: tell others of your commitment and request that they hold you accountable, visualize the results by creating a picture or movie in your mind of you having what you want, and put yourself at a financial risk. Pick some organization you would never give money to and write a check for a substantial amount. Then, give it to a friend with your permission to mail the check if you don't accomplish your goal. Use these kinds of acts and conscious messages to permit your subconscious to work tirelessly to provide you with a solution. If your first action steps and mechanism don't work, choose something else. Never give up on what you want to create."

—⊷⊶—

LOOKING BACK:

Throughout his life, Jake had demanded people trust him unconditionally. His mantra was he didn't care if you liked him, and loving him was optional. But to be in a relationship with him, he had to know you trusted him. To gain others' trust, he created his persona as a loyal, hardworking man of integrity. His superiors depended on him to get things done. He operated within the boundaries and rules of his employers and fully bought into the company's vision and objectives. He took ownership of any responsibility he was given, whether the authority came with it or not. Management noticed his accomplishments. His employers put him on a fast track for promotions, which caused friction between him and those who had been waiting years for promotion. None of this mattered to him, as he intended to become more than either of his parents.

Without knowing the formula for success, which he was teaching around the globe, Jake had accomplished more in his work life than either of his parents. His formula centered around the vow he had made as a child, and his life unfolded from that vow.

His mentor, Tom, had taught a different formula for some 30 years. Tens of thousands of people had lived transformed lives because of his influence. Learning about a proven formula for creating success is an intellectual exercise, which is quite different from an in-depth understanding of the heart (subconscious) level. Once the subconscious is engaged with a clear picture of what you want to create, it begins to bring forth to your consciousness the people, places, opportunities, knowledge, and wisdom needed to realize your objective.

The purpose of the game his audiences participated in was to experience a significant emotional event. When a person has such an event, they look back at their life and ask crucial questions. These questions target their core limiting beliefs, decisions, and worldviews, the lenses through which they experience life. In a room of participants who are all engaged, it is common for one person's significant emotional experience to set off a domino effect resulting in several people having tremendous revelations. These moments can lead to people creating their own breakthrough experiences.

YOUR INTROSPECTIVE CHALLENGE:

1. What goal or objective can you use Jake's formula of success, (C + A = R), to create your desired outcome?

   _____

   _____

   _____

   _____

2. What are the qualities of the person you would like to ask to hold you accountable?

   _____

   _____

   _____

   _____

3. What obstacles are preventing you from working toward the goals you have set or have a vision to achieve?

_____

_____

_____

_____

4. How would you feel when you realize a significant goal?

_____

_____

_____

_____

5. Describe a significant emotional event you experienced and how it transformed your life.

_____

_____

_____

_____

XII

THE ILLUSION OF SEPARATENESS

Whatever affects one directly affects all indirectly.

—Martin Luther King, Jr.

Jake, his brothers, and sisters developed into highly independent individuals growing up in a single-parent home. His mother had raised her seven children, mostly by herself, and whether intentionally or not, they learned personal integrity had greater value than ability. She worked multiple jobs to provide for her family and sacrificed her dreams and aspirations for them. How does a woman abused by her husband of 28 years instill life-giving values into her children when she was raised without them?

She didn't express joy and happiness in her day-to-day life. Often, she was angry, feeling helpless and hopeless. Her strength of character was developed over decades of having to fill both roles of parenting. The unimaginable stress she lived with caused her body to break down, resulting in life-shortening health issues. But none of this got in between her and her love for God. She had faithfully studied the Bible for her entire life and could debate even the best theologians. At an early age, she became a self-disciplined student who loved history and poetry. She was a woman whose heart had been crushed so many times that being in a relationship became a vanishing dream.

Jake had become a version of his mother. He had a chip on his shoulder and believed anyone who wanted to get close had ulterior motives. Eventually, he would be taken advantage of and end up losing from the relationship versus gaining.

When Martin had come out and announced he was gay, Jake didn't have any tools or understanding of how to be in a relationship with gay or lesbian people. All he knew was to judge and reject anyone who rejected him and his beliefs. He felt victimized by his son's announcement and confused about how he could have a gay son when he had raised him in a culture that rejected people like him. He repelled them. Until his son came out, Jake and Grace didn't have anyone close that was a declared gay or lesbian person. *How can I be a father to a gay son?* he wondered.

It wasn't long before Martin had entered the military, which made it easy for Jake to ignore his relationship with his son. After all, he belonged to and was the responsibility of the U.S. Air Force now, and they would make a man out of him. The years passed with little contact between them until Martin disclosed he was in a relationship with a woman. They had met in the military and became close friends while in their field of work. The relationship had become serious, and a wedding date was set. Jake and Grace were thrilled. Finally, their son set himself up for a life that could be filled with joy and happiness. His fiancée was beautiful, funny, and smart, and the two of them seemed overjoyed with getting married and creating a life together.

But, like Jake, Martin didn't have the tools for creating a loving and intimate relationship with his new wife. Within a few short years, their marriage fell apart, and they divorced. Martin was feeling lost and alone, sought out support from gay men whom he identified with. He created a relationship and moved in with a man he felt supported him in ways his wife never did or even could have.

Grace and Jake felt betrayed and rejected by their son, who was, again, living a lifestyle they had judged harshly.

Years passed without much contact between the four of them until Grace came home after attending a women's conference. She said she wanted to invite their son and his partner to Thanksgiving. Grace said she'd heard in her heart that her job was to love her son and not to try to change him. That God was in control, and she needed to be his mother and love him unconditionally. Feeling somewhat resistant, Jake finally agreed to Grace's urging.

Thanksgiving was the beginning of building relationships with both Martin and his partner. The two were like an old married couple, set in their ways, critical of each other, and loved to have fun together. They went on skiing trips, traveled the globe, vacationed on gay cruises, and often hosted parties at their home.

If Martin was happy, why couldn't Jake be happy for him? Grace and Jake spent time with the two of them at their home, and they traveled and spent time with them. Being in a relationship was becoming easier, but there was still distance between them. Martin refused to attend any of the seminars

Grace and Jake were hosting, telling them that it would snow in hell before he subjected himself to that training.

After a rough period between Martin and him, Jake heard a voice in his mind ask, *So, exactly how much time have you spent on the cross, Jake?*

It was such a piercing question, and Jake had to examine what it meant and why it came up. A realization came over him that he judged Martin for being gay because he believed God would judge him for having a son that was gay. The clarity around this question provided him with deep peace, and he knew what he had to do.

Within two weeks, Jake flew to Texas and met with Martin. He shared with him his epiphany, saying, "All I want is to have a father-son relationship with you. If you want the same, then let's begin to work together."

The two of them embraced and sobbed tears of joy for what they were about to create together. That single act and admission changed everything between Martin and him. Times together became more fun and fulfilling. Both sets of parents finally met and enjoyed supporting their sons in the life they were creating together.

One day, out of the blue, Martin called from Sydney, Australia. He was emotional and had a difficult time as he shared what he was going through. By the end of the call, Martin said, "I think I need to come to one of your seminars. My life isn't working, and I need help."

Jake's heart pounded in his chest with excitement. He welcomed him to come to the next seminar and explained he would be in San Francisco, but his mother would be there for support.

That weekend seminar was a difficult training for Martin. He was a practicing atheist and felt that the facilitator was introducing far too much religion by talking about Jesus during the weekend. By the conclusion of the second day, Martin was ready to quit and not return. Grace intervened and shared that there was an exercise on the last day she would love to do with him. She convinced him with some cajoling to return and do, at least, that exercise with her.

Together, Grace and her son shared moments of pain, release, and love that was deeper than anything they had experienced as mother and son. Their time together during the three days became a foundation that they built on and have created a deeply loving mother and son relationship.

Within a relatively short time, Martin decided he should attend the next level seminar, which was more intensive. Though he wanted to avoid the personal and intense self-reflection required and let the pain of his past remain in the past, he weighed the risks and chose to attend.

It would be an understatement to say that Grace and Jake were excited for him to experience what they had only a few years earlier.

A tragedy struck in the family of Jake's co-facilitator. His family suffered the loss of their father, and his co-facilitator would not be able to attend the next seminar, the very one that Jake's son would be attending. In all fairness, Jake thought it best to call his son and ask him to reschedule because he planned to stay home for the first three days of the seminar so Martin could take a deep dive into his past and wrestle with his demons without concern his father was in the room. But with his co-facilitator staying home with his family to mourn his loss, Jake couldn't leave the lead facilitator by herself. His son refused to reschedule, saying it wasn't a coincidence and that he was coming anyway.

The lead facilitator worked out a schedule with Jake to be out of the room during the high risk and emotional exercises. Additionally, she agreed to maintain Martin's privacy related to who his father was during the seminar.

Though his co-facilitator would never divulge his son's experiences during those moments when he was out of the room, Jake could tell by the shift in Martin's state he was taking himself on and creating transformative breakthroughs.

The day they spent on the high ropes course spoke volumes about the entire team's growth after only four days. This was a day that took committed teamwork by the participants and staff to create success without an injury-causing incident. The participants would be 40 feet off the ground much of the day, and they needed to work as one because they held each other's lives in their hands.

The end of the day in the redwood forest was a particularly poignant time for Jake, Grace, and Martin. The team had completed The Wall exercise that both Grace and Jake had experienced. This exercise had resulted in Jake connecting all the common themes and threads of his emotional wounds and betrayal in his life. He saw how he had created himself to be a one-person show in business and personal life. The clarity of that moment in time was so intense, Jake felt both broken by and free from his past.

As the team surrounded each other, sobbing, laughing, and cheering for their accomplishments throughout the day, Grace and Jake noticed a completely different state in their son. He was exuding joy with a capital J. Never had they seen him so completely engaged with others, expressing through his tears and hugs how much they had come to mean to him.

Grace looked at Jake and said, "You can't stand here and decide not to go to your son and let him know how much you love him."

Her statement sounded a bit harsh, but Jake knew her meaning. Besides, she had no knowledge of the privacy agreement that the facilitators had with their son. Jake approached his son, who immediately reached out and hugged him with the most heartfelt connection Jake and he had shared in more than a decade.

The connection made between a father and son was what both had longed for. They had taken themselves on and done the hard-introspective work to get to that point in their relationship, and the rewards were tremendous. Not only was Jake seeing his son in a different light, but he also saw others differently. It wasn't long before Jake and Grace noticed they were attracting more gay and lesbian people in their space. For Jake, he connected with gay men and was effective in coaching them to breakthrough during the intense seminar. Lesbians seemed to seek him out as a father figure to help them through their heartbreak of not having a loving and connected father during their formative years.

You might wonder, was this a coincidence? If you asked Jake today, he would tell you his state, for most of his life, repelled people in need of emotional support. Once he shifted and fell in love with himself and humanity, a pathway opened for those in need of connection and support to find their way to him. Even his co-facilitators noticed the difference during the seminars. Jake attracted more of the emotionally wounded participants into his space versus the other facilitators. He made it safe for them to be open, transparent, and vulnerable as he was with them. Together, they created deep revelations and breakthroughs that helped launch the participants into a new and exciting future.

From his experience working with tens of thousands of people worldwide, more live life in survival mode than they do from passion and purpose. When trying to survive, a person exists day to day, possibly having wishes, goals, and unrealized desires. Providing shelter, food, and safety becomes his or her daily priority. It isn't long before their consciousness no longer supports thoughts of abundant time, liberty, travel, a career, owning a home on an acreage, or a luxury vehicle. Others are viewed as better than, better off, smarter, more educated, and richer, and they get more than their share of the breaks in life. Being in survival mode creates an illusion of separateness in his or her mind.

There is a concept known as the illusion of separateness and the reality of oneness. It means that one does not see other humans as a being created in the same image. We first see their color, race, sex, nationality, religion, sexual preference, political views, level of education and degrees, ethnicity, and more before seeing their humanity. It is as though we are two vastly different islands in the ocean, separated by a vast chasm that seems impassable.

In the Pacific Ocean near the island of Maui, there is another island, Kahoolawe. Its highest point is 1,477 feet above sea level, and it gets around 26 inches of rain per year, making it a dry and arid island. During the Second World War, the U.S. Armed Forces used this island as a training ground and bombing range. Forty-five years later, the U.S. Navy stopped using the island for live-fire practice.[10] Kahoolawe became a bombed-out island versus a thriving and populous island of the Hawaiian Islands.

If you were to float in a raft between the islands of Maui and Kahoolawe, you would notice the obvious differences.

There is a thriving population on Maui who lives there and supports one of the greatest tourist destination points on earth. There are skyscraper hotels, lush jungle-like hiking locations, sugar cane fields, pineapple fields, golf courses, palm trees, beautiful gardens, and homes. Along the coastline is the winding Hana Highway, waterfalls, two dormant volcanoes—and more.

You would see Kahoolawe, one of the four islands that make up Maui County, in the opposite direction. However, the island of Kahoolawe appears to be a completely different representation of the Hawaiian Islands. After being used for a bombing range for almost 50 years, there isn't much left on this island. Craters mark the landscape, and unexploded ordinances may be buried in the ground. Little vegetation grows, and it lacks an abundance of freshwater. Tourists don't visit the island—it is an abandoned landmass in the Pacific Ocean that has little value except to the native Hawaiian Islanders who have permission to use it for spiritual and cultural purposes.

Using the concept of the illusion of separateness and the reality of oneness, if by some incredible act or event, the ocean between the islands were to begin to drain away with the raft dropping in elevation, you would notice more likeness between the two islands. Below the water level, each island has a commonality and appears much the same. Should all the water drain away and your raft settles to the ocean floor, you would see that all around the scenery is the same. Below the surface, the islands are more alike than they are dissimilar above the surface. And these islands are connected to the earth's entire surface.

So, what has this to do with humanity? On our surface, as human beings, we may appear quite different from each other. Our sex, height, weight, race, religion, education, sexual preference, and level of wealth seem to make us different and separate from each other. But at a deeper level, we are much the same. Yes, our DNA is somewhat different from each other, but we bleed red. We have similar nervous systems, and we have a brain to think with, feelings, emotions, childhood wounds, parents, aunts, uncles, siblings, cousins, wants, desires, fears—and so much more that is common to humanity. What if, below our surface, we are connected like the islands?

Maybe it's at a spiritual or a universal level connection. In many ancient writings, such as that of Mark 12:31, it is commanded to "love your neighbor as yourself."[11] Doesn't that mean we cannot love anyone to any depth greater than the love we have for ourselves? If that connection exists, and I believe it does, then what we do to and think about ourselves, and act on, influences everyone around us.

Mark 12:31: It is commanded to "love your neighbor as yourself."

Imagine this incredible and vast universe we live in is like a giant web. Each of us has our place in the web, but the Creator of the web is aware of every thought we have and the acts we perform, all of which create vibrations. The Creator immediately picks up the slightest vibration or movement or projection of thought, and a shift begins to happen in the web. My thoughts, your thoughts, and our collective actions are impacting each other in ways we may be unaware of and haven't imagined.

Have you ever wondered why, after only four years as president of the United States, every president appears to have aged far more than he should have in his short time in office? If this happened to a few of the presidents, we'd think it was a coincidence. But it happens to each of them. If half the population of the United States is focusing and projecting their thoughts and prayers as negative energy against the President, then, given the concept of being connected, the reality of oneness, it stands to reason they might age more quickly.

What about the rest of the world's population? If 30% of the world's people do the same, imagine what that kind of focused negative energy force against one man or woman could have. And what about the people who are holding these negative thoughts consistently in their conscious minds? Negativity breeds more negativity. Soon, a person who projects these kinds of thoughts and vibrations separates themselves from others and begins to create greater stress in their body. Our healthcare system is overwhelmed with people who suffer from mental and physical illness directly attributed to their negative stress levels. Their critical inner voice has a stronghold, which they have not learned to overcome. Dreams and aspirations no longer live in their consciousness because everything they ever wanted seems impossible.

LOOKING BACK:

How different would your life become if you could see others as they are versus as you are? They are, after all, people like you. Take a moment to think of a person with whom you have a strained or seriously damaged relationship. While holding their name and image in your consciousness, say these statements out loud and to yourself:

Like me, this person has dreams and fears.

Like me, this person is searching for love.

Like me, this person has deep desires.

Like me, this person has experienced pain.

And like me, this person wants many of the things I want.

People from around the world want the same core things—to love, to be loved, to be accepted, to be heard, and to be understood. When we experience these things, we are filled up to overflowing and will do everything in our power to share our gain and gifts with others.

Jake had become a transformed leader with a mission to make it possible for everyone who crossed his path to have the same opportunities for revelations and breakthroughs that he had. These opportunities resulted in individuals and corporations creating a culture of passion and purpose, which could result in a more significant and fulfilled life and company growth with a greater return to its stakeholders.

Being experienced in connecting with individuals and providing them a safe and confidential space, Jake became a highly sought-out coach and group intensive facilitator. His decades of living the illusion of separateness made him the perfect guide who knew the way to the reality of oneness. He knew of the pitfalls, mind fields, and excuses that individuals and corporations used to justify playing a small game of life. His experience of being one of them made him a material expert, a credible counsel, and a trusted coach.

YOUR INTROSPECTIVE CHALLENGE:

1. When you gaze into a mirror, who do you see? Do you see a single individual or an intricate member of the universal web, who has a vital role to live out?

   _____
   _____
   _____
   _____

2. How do you view others as they relate to the illusion of separateness?

_____

_____

_____

_____

3. If you had the opportunity to create revelations and breakthroughs, what action would you take first, second, and third?

_____

_____

_____

_____

4. Imagine you are in the rowboat, and on one side of the boat are broken relationships, and on the other side are opportunities. What steps would you take so you could have both restored relationships and as many of the opportunities as you wanted?

_____

_____

_____

_____

FINAL EXERCISE:

This is the final exercise for you at this stage of your journey. On a clean sheet of paper, write down all the things you would accomplish if time, education, skill, and money were not issues. Think of the outrageous things you might do or become, such as:

- Take a trip into space.
- Discover a cure for the next pandemic.
- Heal all the broken relationships in the world.
- Create world peace.
- Eliminate world hunger.
- Run for and be elected to Congress.
- Start your dream company.
- Marry your dream spouse.
- Write your book.

If time, education, skill, and money were not an issue, what would your list look like?

Stop here.

Complete your list in the next sixty seconds, without letting your negative self-talk override what you write down.

Imagine you only have the next 24 hours to live, and you want to restore any damaged or broken relationships you may have with the most important people in your life. But, at the end of those 24 hours, your time on this earth is ended. Whatever you don't restore will remain in the hearts and minds of those people.

Stop here.

Write the names of the most important people you want to restore relationships with. Take 30 seconds right now and write those names as if your time is running out.

Stop writing.

Look at your list of people. Does it include a parent, child, friend, sibling, aunt, uncle, boss, co-worker, God, a member of your church, or a stranger? Is your name on the list? If not, why not? Odds are the number one reason you have struggled in your life is because you don't love and respect yourself. Throughout your lifetime, you have unconsciously trained others how to treat you by the way you treat and speak of yourself. Isn't it time you forgive yourself for all those things you have done to hurt yourself? Forgiveness doesn't have to be hard. It is a choice made so you can be freed from the self-imposed prison. Forgiving yourself may be the most difficult action you take, but it makes forgiving others easier and easier each time you make that choice. You have everything to gain—your dreams, goals, aspirations, restored relationships, and love of self and others.

The realization why we don't have what we want can be as freeing as when we have what we want. It brings clarity, focus, courage, and commitment forward in us. The resistance you may be experiencing likely is generated from within yourself. You may be in resistance to your dreams and aspirations. When you integrate the lessons contained in *Despite Me*, you gain the power to be in control of your destiny. You'll have the power to create all you desire. The only person to hold responsible for every result you produce is you! Being in your way leads to a life of heartbreak and disappointment! When you become crystal clear with your commitment to the kind of life you desire, your results are assured. As you look back over this journey, can you see how the broken pieces of Jake's life have come into focus, much like inside a kaleidoscope, looking more beautiful than ever imagined? With each broken piece fitting, perfectly together and revealing the beauty of life, that shapes a stained-glass window into his history.

You have the power to create these kinds of results, but it takes commitment and gut-wrenching self-introspection to reveal all the darkness and hardened places of your heart. Once you uncover these painful wounds, you can heal them. No one else can. From time to time, you may wander away from your dreams and goals. Know that deep within your being, there is a longing for whole and complete healing, and when you try once more, you are starting from a new place and a stronger state. With each new beginning, you become more courageous, confident, and committed. You are, after all, on a mission to restore your authentic heart.

Take massive action today and reap the benefits of a life lived from love.

ABOUT THE AUTHOR

John Edwards is committed to creating transformational leaders using his books, seminars, and facilitation, coaching, and being an example of successful, intentional character development. He believes by helping adults overcome their limiting beliefs, make better decisions, and shift their worldviews that they, too, will return to their families and begin to create generational change.

Growing up in a culture of poverty and victim mindsets, John struggled for decades to find his way and know who he was as a youth and a man. His experiences of abandonment, sexual molestation, and betrayal were the foundation for his inability to trust anyone with his heart.

For more than 30 years, John poured himself into the lumber and wood products industry in Oregon and Washington. Leading hundreds of workers and supervisors, he gained their trust and respect for what he could produce and his steady hand at the helm. But it was how he showed up in the world that was not working, and he came to realize this when his last employer sold the company without consulting him.

John retired from this industry in the year 2000, committed to making a change before something unthinkable happened. He immersed himself into his character transformation.

John's years of heart-wrenching efforts in his transformation have paid huge dividends for his family, businesses, and himself. He is now a highly sought out speaker, trainer, executive coach, life coach, seminar facilitator, and producer. John lives his life passionately while fulfilling his purpose.

An influential and inspiring leader, John trains leaders inside corporations, associations, churches, and the military, leading them to develop their leaders in new approaches and techniques. He has facilitated thousands of people in corporate and personal leadership and spiritual development seminars. He produces and facilitates multi-day workshops globally, including in the United States, Europe, Canada, Australia, and Asia. John holds several national and board certifications, making him uniquely qualified to guide others through their transformational journey.

ACKNOWLEDGMENTS

In honor of my mentors who stood in the gap when I was too young to be on my own and didn't know how to find my way, you have my eternal gratitude. Your influence in my life supported me in reframing my father's relationship to overcome my unconscious programming of abandonment and betrayal. I had no idea that his choices would lead to your mentoring, which guided my path beyond victimhood and poverty to a life of passion and purpose.

Father-in-law, Walter Perry King, your family context of love and acceptance was so opposite of the culture I grew up in that I didn't know how to handle what you were offering me. Though it took me a long time to understand a father's love could look different, you never gave up on me.

Employer, Fritz Marvel, you treated me like your own and taught me all the things a father would teach his son. From you, I learned how to build buildings, lay plumbing, and electrical lines, fell timber, hand hew logs, chop more firewood than I could ever imagine, chase down boats during a storm, clean and wax floors to a mirror shine, cut fir bows for Christmas decorations, and so much more. You were direct and loving, and I always knew where I stood with you.

Manager and employer, Jerry Scott, you taught me everything you knew about lumber and manufacturing. As a young man with little experience, you believed in me and gave me my first management position, which led to becoming a plant manager within three years and managing multiple plants within eight years.

My first trainer, coach, and mentor, Brian Klemmer, who introduced me to personal and leadership development, shook me to my core. In that experience, I chose to transform my character completely. Under your mentorship, I gained my love of humanity: I could never have imagined, love, and acceptance of myself, which I now extend to others. When I asked to train as a facilitator in your company, you didn't hesitate to invite me into your inner circle. Though you have been gone for years, your work lives on through me and so many others whose lives you touched.

NOTES

1   Prov. 23:7 /nkjv/
2   Rom. 12:2
3   Luke 6:45
4   Groth, Aimee. "You're The Average Of The Five People You
    Spend The Most Time With." Business Insider. Business
    Insider, July 24, 2012. https://www.businessinsider.com/
    jim-rohn-youre-the-average-of-the-five-people-you-spend-
    the-most-time-with-2012-7.
5   "Theta Wave." Wikipedia. Wikimedia Foundation, January
    12, 2021. https://en.wikipedia.org/wiki/Theta_wave.
6   Minds, Changing. Values Development, 2002. http://
    changingminds.org/explanations/values/values_
    development.htm.
7   Minds, Changing. "Morris Massey." Wikipedia. Wikimedia
    Foundation, June 4, 2020. https://en.wikipedia.org/wiki/
    Morris_Massey.

8 Tan PB. Evaluating the "unconscious in a dream" between Sigmund Freud and the Buddhist Tipitaka. *JIABU*. 2016;9(1):36-46 | ch. VIII, p. 113

9 Hill, Napoleon. "The Power of the Master Mind." Think and Grow Rich: Chapter 10. Power of the Master Mind (The Ninth Step toward Riches), 1938. https://sacred-texts.com/nth/tgr/tgr15.htm.

10 Data Book, State of Hawaii. "Kahoolawe." Wikipedia. Wikimedia Foundation, July 2, 2020. https://en.wikipedia.org/wiki/Kahoolawe.

11 Mark 12:31

About Life Quest Seminars

Mission: To lead, inspire and influence men and women to encounter, experience and restore their authentic heart.

Bringing three distinct training mechanisms together, John and his team created a unique training modality and experience. Participants of Life Quest Seminars gain more profound clarity and understanding of the truths of who they are and the obstacles and illusions that continue to prevent them from creating their best life. Each participant will be battle-tested, armed with tools, and strengthened to understand that they do not have to go it alone. Our graduates can expect to experience release and renewal during the training and leave feeling engaged, empowered, and inspired to live passionately in their purpose, having restored their authentic heart.

To learn more, go to:
www.lifequestseminars.com

Schedule a strategy session with John and learn how your investment in team and leadership development pays maximum returns to the individuals, organization and stakeholders.

Call: 1-(800)-260-3685 (office)
Email: info@lifequestseminars.com